The Federal Siege At
Ruby
Ridge

In Our Own Words

The Federal Siege At

Ruby Ridge

In Our Own Words

By Randy and Sara Weaver

Ruby Ridge, Inc.
Marion, MT

Published by:
Ruby Ridge, Inc.
P.O. Box 1101
Marion, MT 59925

ISBN 0-9664334-0-8

Library of Congress Catalog Card Number 98-66639

Second Printing

Back cover photo of Randy Weaver by Robbie McClaran
Back cover photo of Sara Weaver, Front Cover Photo and
recent family photo by Bill Henry
Color separations by Digital Planet
Text design and layout by Linda Gross

Printed in the United States of America

In Loving Memory of

Vicki and Sam Weaver

**Murdered by Federal Agents
At Ruby Ridge
August 1992**

Table of Contents

Foreword

By Colonel James "Bo" Gritz

Every now and then the best of government runs amok. On rare occasion the people respond to reestablish their proper master-servant relationship with such a Frankenstein. When they fail, tyranny prevails. 19 April 1775 marks the "shot heard around the world," when soldiers arrived at Lexington to disarm the American militia. In March 1968, the Americal Division moved on the Vietnamese village of My Lai. There to protect the populace from Communism, they murdered more than 300 women, children and infants. Another such instance of official abuse began at Ruby Ridge, Boundary County, Idaho in August 1992. A "Special Operations Group" maneuvering to apprehend Randy Weaver, shot 14-year old Sam in the back as he ran for home, having already killed his Yellow Lab, Striker. The ambush team then gunned-down one of its own, as William Degan, the most decorated U.S. Marshal, crossed a burst of fire from a silent sub-machine gun.

Governor Cecil Andrus, declaring a state of "extreme emergency," surrendered jurisdiction to federal authority. Dressed and acting in the fashion of terrorists, hundreds of federal militarized police massed with weapons of war on the Weaver cabin vowing "No one will come off that hill alive!" Under "modified shoot on sight rules of engagement," Delta Force trained FBI snipers, without warning, opened fire on Randy Weaver from behind, as he prepared to look in on his dead son. A friend, Kevin Harris was grievously wounded running into the cabin. Worst of all, Vicki Weaver was shot through the face, clutching infant, Elisheba, while holding the door open for her beloved husband and daughter, Sara.

More than a week the two wounded men and three little girls huddled behind the plywood walls of their hand-built home, convinced a predator government would kill them. A 750-pound shotgun equipped robot was positioned at the door to frighten the family with such broadcast taunts as: "We are having blueberry pancakes for breakfast. What are you fixing for your family Mrs. Weaver?" Domestic animals died from neglect and were destroyed when neighbors were forced to evacuate their homes. Jack, a friend and part-time employer, higher up on the mountain, averted a helicopter carrying a fuel cell, that he and a TV cameraman were certain was meant to burn the Weavers out.

As if in a Rambo movie, I was called by the FBI to record a statement to the former Green Beret Demolition Sergeant, Randy Weaver. Millions of Americans sacrificed life, limb and liberty to safeguard our nation and citizens from the uniformed terror assembled on Ruby Ridge. There was never a question of over-reaction. It was clear to me the government did not intend to take any prisoners, but getting to the Weavers wasn't easy. The Feds didn't want any outside interference or witnesses, but reconsidered when served with a citizen's arrest.

The valley FBI headquarters looked like a combat firebase with military helicopters, armored vehicles, large tents, mess facilities, motorpools, communication center, heavily armed troops in battledress, and a guarded command post. National Guard patrols prowled the perimeter, while the elite Hostage Response Team ruled the roost. Dick Rogers, a Second Lieutenant in Vietnam, was "king of the mountain" as described by Gene Glenn, the FBI Chief Agent-in-Charge. Rogers' tactical CP, littered with garbage, was down the trail and around from the Weaver cabin about 150-yards. Rogers reminded me of the Star Wars villain, Darth Vader, dressed out in full body armor, helmet, camouflage, and weapon. His 100-man unit mirrored their commander except for M-16 machine guns, Remington 700 sniper rifles and no-see-me "Ghillie" suits.

I first learned that Vicki had been killed when Randy shouted from the cabin that the FBI was "keeping it a secret." Darth Vader met me as I left the hilltop. His arms were extended defensively as he stated: "We *targeted* Vicki Weaver because the psychiatrist profiled her as the maternal head of the family, who would kill the children before allowing them to surrender." At the bottom, Gene

Glenn inquired: "What are we going to do about Vicki Weaver?" When I responded that her parents were present and I wouldn't allow her death to remain a secret, Glenn asked if he could be the one to tell them. There was never a doubt about Vicki being purposely shot until after the siege was over and a disgraceful cover-up began.

Had I not been a soldier, I would hope to have served in the FBI. Even as My Lai was not representative of the American Military, neither was Ruby Ridge a credit to agents whose motto is *"Fidelity, Integrity, Bravery."* The difference is that Army Lt. William Calley was charged with murder, while FBI sniper Lon Horiuchi was awarded a medal! In America everyone is supposed to be afforded equal protection under the law. I was appalled at the extremely vicious attitude of Dick Rogers. There were no Efrem Zimbalist, Jr.-types in his HRT. The unit was the same as combat commando teams I have led. They were there to hurt instead of help their quarry. As further evidence of this craving for no survivors, Rogers informed me after Harris was evacuated, and I had carried Vicki's body from the cabin, that if Weaver and his three girls didn't surrender by noon the next day, they would be "taken out!" There was no reason for such a deadline in lieu of steady progress.

No doubt if the rest of the Weavers and Kevin Harris had perished along with Sam and Vicki, the case would have been quickly closed, but thousands of people prayed otherwise. I felt inspired that there was a greater purpose possible if Randy and Kevin could be brought to trial. It was essential for justice that they not only survive the siege, but have representation capable of winning in court. I telephoned Gerry Spence, briefed him on the situation, and asked him to defend Randy Weaver, which he gave his word to do. In superb style Spence proved defendant innocence and assigned government guilt in Degan's death. Harris left a free man, while it took more than three years for the Department of Justice to award Sara, Rachel, and Elisheba $3.2-million for the wrongful death of their Mother. More than the Weavers, all of America won with their survival and court victory—the monster within government was stayed for a season!

Many books, articles, and even a TV movie were made about Ruby Ridge by people who weren't there. This book is authored by Randy and Sara Weaver, the only people who know a fullness of the truth. Awareness of the facts surrounding Ruby Ridge can help keep the government in its proper place—and with God's Grace grant us all true justice!

Bo Gritz, America's most decorated Green Beret Commander, was featured by General William Westmoreland as "The" American Soldier. Gritz went in rescue of U.S. POWs. He negotiated a peaceful end to the deadly siege at Ruby Ridge.

Acknowledgements

We can't begin to acknowledge and thank everyone who has provided prayers, support, and friendship, not only during the assault on our home, but also over the past several years since the tragedy occurred. There are numerous people however, that we want to thank from the bottom of our hearts, for without you, our lives would now be meaningless.

First and foremost we wish to extend thanks to our family, the Weavers and the Jordisons. They have been an inspiration of strength and love for all of us. They too, have become victims of a system out of control, with no recourse for the loss of their loved ones. Their continued support has meant so much to us over the years as we try to get on with our lives. We love you all.

I (Randy) would like to personally thank my wonderful daughters. They, who have had to experience more than any child should have to bear, have done so with honesty, integrity, and a strength and faith much greater than mine. When I sat in jail wanting to die their presence and love was the only thing that kept me going. I love you girls.

Thanks to Kevin Harris, who is like a son to me, and a brother to Sara, Sam, Rachel, and Elisheba. Kevin, your strength, courage, and friendship as a part of our family are worth more than you will ever know.

We thank Linda Gross, Randy's girlfriend, for her loyalty, love and understanding. Also much appreciation for her devotion to helping us make this book a reality. You have a heart of gold and we all love you.

I (Sara) want to thank my fiancé, David Cooper. You have stood by my family and I from day one, offering comfort, encouragement and support. Your love and patience has pulled me through many rough times and helped me to realize that life can hold joy and happiness as well as grief and sorrow. You are one of the few honorable, kind and unselfish people I have ever met. I love you.

We must give a very special thanks to Colonel James "Bo" Gritz and Jack McLamb, who literally were willing to put their lives on the line, rather than allow the FBI to murder the rest of us, as we believe they intended to.

An extremely special thank you is in order to Gerry Spence and Co-counsel Chuck Peterson, Gary Gilman, David Nevin, and Ellison Matthews. Through their combined efforts, expertise, donated time, and expense they exposed what the government has frantically tried to cover up from the beginning. The truth. Thanks also to our family attorney, Mike Mumma.

We would like to extend thanks to all the members of the jury. Your willingness to listen to the truth and thus realizing the attack on our family was premeditated confirms that even against all odds, the American justice system guaranteed by our constitution can work. We have a ways to go before justice will be done, but the cornerstone has been laid by all of you. Thank you.

Our sincere gratitude to all our friends and neighbors who stood vigil at the roadblock the week of the siege. As much as the press tried to demonize you, your actions and perseverance portrayed the love and concern shared by most Americans toward their fellow man. We are truly convinced your presence had a lot to do with the reason our lives were spared, and we are now able to share the truth with the rest of the world through this book.

We would also like to thank Senator Craig and Representative Chenowith, from Idaho. Also, Senator Grassley from Iowa and Senator Spectre, Chairman of the Investigative Committee, for conducting the hearings on the Federal Raid on Ruby Ridge. We appreciate the time and effort spent by the committee to get the truth. We hope you will display the same diligence to insure that FBI sniper Lon Horiuchi and U.S. Marshal Larry Cooper are charged with murder in the first degree, after the facts come out in Horiuchi's manslaughter trial. We hope you will display the courage and common sense that Americans expect from their elected officials, and have the medals revoked that were issued to the U.S. Marshals for the "courage" shown by shooting a 14-year-old boy in the back as he ran for home.

We would also like to thank and offer our condolences to the family of Lorenze Caduff, former proprietors of the Deep Creek Inn in Naples, Idaho.

Thanks to our many friends and fellow patriots who have offered their prayers and support to us over the past several years. We have received thousands of letters from people all over the country sharing their condolences and apologies for the atrocities perpetrated by the government on our family.

A special thanks to all of our close friends who have always been there for us. Names are too numerous to mention, but you know who you are. You will never know how much your words and moral support mean to us.

Finally, we would like to thank our ghostwriter Steve Douglas and the many people who helped make this book possible.

We thank you all.

C HAPTER

1

Introduction

If you laid all our laws end to end, there would be no end.

--Arthur Baer

The purpose of this book is to tell you why we believe the tragedy at Ruby Ridge occurred and why we also believe it could happen again...maybe even to you or someone you know. This book is not "politically correct" or "sugarcoated", but then the tragedy at Ruby Ridge wasn't either.

There are those people who believe Ruby Ridge occurred because of paranoia on both sides, the federal government and our family. We disagree and say that what the federal government did up there only proves *their* paranoia and none on the part of our family. Shortly after we surrendered, federal agents asked Sara how she felt about what I had taught her concerning the government. Sara replied that the government had just proved that what I had told her was true.

We are not anti-government. We are anti *bad* government. At any given time there are portions of our government that are not acting according to the people's wishes. Sometimes they are even acting unlawfully. We want to trust the government but we have learned that is not always a good idea. This is a thought-provoking story. The most we can ask is that each of you come to your own conclusions.

There is an old saying, *"When the government fears the people you have freedom, but when the people fear the government you have slavery."* That is still the case today and many people do, and have, every reason to fear their government. The agents responsible for Ruby Ridge have not admitted to the truth to this day. It's very obvious to us why they continue to double-talk and cover-up. If they were to admit what actually happened, they would be in prison. It appears as though most police agents must be immune from perjury. That is so very wrong and very scary. There should be a grassroots movement to have that changed!

Many of the people whom government agencies approach to become snitches have committed crimes in the past and are offered immunity by agreeing to help catch other "criminals". These snitches are under an umbrella of pressure to produce results in order to get paid and they

2

will go to whatever means necessary to achieve those results. Even if that means actually helping to create a crime so as to cause someone else to go down in the justice system. This is called entrapment and this is exactly what happened in my case. Entrapment is illegal, yet Gus Magisono is still a free man and presumably continues to snitch for the ATF while three people are dead because of his illegal actions.

People should understand that the news media can make you out to be anything they want with the use of "buzzwords". These are words that are designed to evoke a certain reaction. Words like "radical" or "white supremacist" are designed to create a negative or sinister image of a person. Various government agents and the media have labeled us as white supremacists. To set the record straight, we are not, and never have been supremacists. We can't help the fact that we were born white. A *supremacist* is a person who believes he or she is superior over another because of their race, religion or even social status.

You can consider us *separatists* both religiously and politically speaking.

A religious separatist believes in freedom of religion and believes that he has the right to worship in his own way. Also, part of that religious separatist belief is that the different races should not intermarry. As far as that belief is concerned, you could be black, white, red, or yellow.

Politically speaking, if it were possible, we would separate ourselves from much of the control that our government has placed us under. The first Europeans that came to this country didn't call themselves Pilgrims, Puritans, or Christians, but rather they called themselves separatists. They were separating from the established political and religious system of Europe. They were tired of the persecution at the hands of that system. After many years of studying, we realized that our system today isn't all that dissimilar to the systems in Europe in the past. The main difference would be that our present system is much larger and more powerful, and seems impossible to escape.

Davy Crockett once said that a good lawmaker is one that makes as few laws as possible. That has changed over the years. Lawmakers now feel that the more laws they make, the better they are doing their job. They brag about how many laws they have helped to pass and believe each law they pass is another "feather in their cap". They just can't understand or don't care, that the American people are getting fed up with it.

The more numerous the laws, the more corrupt the state.
      --Tacitus

If nature had as many laws as the State, God Himself could not reign over it.
      --Ludwig Boerne

Legality is killing us.
      --J. G. Viennet

Thousands of American patriots have died to insure the freedom we take for granted in this country. A *patriot* is simply a person who loves and serves his country. Anyone who has a will to live is a *survivalist*. Anyone who takes pride in his or her heritage or ethnic culture can be a *separatist*. These are not bad words. Don't be fooled by media buzzwords. Seek the truth and the truth shall set you free.

2

Chronology of Events

*The essence of government is power, and power, lodged
as it must be in human hands, will ever be liable to abuse.*

--James Madison

The following is an abbreviated chronology of events regarding the Ruby Ridge debacle.

~~~~~~~~~~~~~~~~~~

- **July 1986** – Weaver unwittingly befriended by ATF undercover snitch.

~~~~~~~~~~~~~~~~~~

- **October 1989** - After three years of friendship Weaver agrees to sell two sawed off shotguns to ATF snitch.

~~~~~~~~~~~~~~~~~~

- **June 1990** - ATF agents threaten Weaver with six Federal firearm violations unless he agrees to cooperate with them and become a snitch. Weaver refuses.

- **December 1990** - Because of Weaver's refusal to cooperate a Federal Grand Jury in Boise indicts him on charges of manufacturing and possessing illegal sawed off shotguns.

~~~~~~~~~~~~~~~~~~

- **January 17, 1991** - Weaver and his wife Vicki are arrested on Ruby Creek Road leading to their north Idaho cabin by undercover agents posing as a couple with a broken down vehicle.

- **January 18, 1991** - Weaver is released from jail after using his property as collateral to post a $10,000 promissory bond. Court date is set for February 19, 1991.

- **February 7, 1991** - Weaver is sent a notice that his trial has been changed to March 20, 1991 when it was actually reset for February 20, 1991.

6

- **February 22, 1991** - Weaver failed to show for trial scheduled in Moscow, Idaho and a bench warrant is issued when U.S. Marshals deny sending him a notice with the wrong date. U.S. Marshals begin an 18-month surveillance of his cabin.

~~~~~~~~~~~~~~~~~~~

- **August 21, 1992** - On surveillance around Weaver's cabin, marshals unexpectedly encounter Weaver, his son Samuel, and Kevin Harris. During a shootout Deputy U.S. Marshal William Degan, Samuel Weaver, and Samuel Weaver's dog Striker are killed. Federal agents, state and local police, and National Guard troops converge on the scene.

- **August 22, 1992** - FBI snipers begin firing at the Weavers wounding Randy and Kevin and killing Vicki.

- **August 23, 1992** - FBI agents find Samuel Weaver's body in the guest shed and federal murder charges are filed against Kevin Harris. Weaver is charged with assaulting a federal officer.

- **August 24, 1992** - Sam Weaver's grandparents learn of his death on the national news because FBI agents guarding them had not released the information. Agents begin broadcasting audio taped messages from relatives and friends begging Weaver to pick up the telephone being held by a robot outside the door.

- **August 25, 1992** - Police begin arresting protesters and Weaver supporters that have weapons in their vehicles.

- **August 26, 1992** - Former Green Beret Colonel James "Bo" Gritz offers to speak to Weaver.

- **August 27, 1992** - Syndicated radio commentator Paul Harvey makes a plea for Weaver and Harris to surrender. He also pleads for them to retrieve the telephone from the robot.

- **August 28, 1992** - Authorities allow Gritz to speak to Weaver. The FBI now has to admit to the public that Vicki Weaver has been killed.

- **August 29, 1992** - Gerry Spence offers to look into the case and represent Weaver if he believes Weaver is innocent. Harris offers to give himself up if all charges are dropped against Weaver.

- **August 30, 1992** - Harris surrenders unconditionally and admits that he shot Degan in self-defense. Weaver allows Gritz and a family friend to take his wife's body from the cabin.

- **August 31, 1992** - The standoff ends. Weaver is arrested and taken to Boise and Vicki's parents take Sara, Rachel, and Elisheba back to Iowa.

- **September 10, 1992** - Preliminary court hearings begin in Boise.

- **September 11, 1992** – U.S. Marshal Larry Cooper testifies that Weaver shot at them during the August 21, 1992 shootout. Hearing is discontinued and grand jury indictments are brought against Weaver and Harris.

- **October 1, 1992** - A grand jury releases a new ten-count indictment against Weaver and Harris. These counts include murder, assault, firearms, and harboring a fugitive.

- **November 10, 1992** - Federal agents claim they expected to find bombs, booby traps, grenades, and bunkers at Weaver's cabin.

- **November 17, 1992** - Defense attorneys unsuccessfully ask a judge to dismiss the grand jury indictments.

~~~~~~~~~~~~~~~~~~

- **April 13, 1993** - Jury selection begins. Seven women and five men are eventually seated on the jury.

- **April 19, 1993** – Branch Davidian Compound in Waco, Texas leveled by fire. Over 80 men, women and children perish. Many of the government agents involved were also present at Ruby Ridge.

- **June 10, 1993** - Prosecutors call their last witness and attorneys for Weaver and Harris rest their case without calling a single witness.

- **June 15, 1993** - Both sides give Closing arguments and jurors begin deliberations the following day.

- **July 8, 1993** - The jury acquits Harris on all charges and Weaver is convicted only of a "failure to appear" charge.

- **December 18, 1993** – Randy Weaver is released from jail and returns to live in Iowa with his daughters.

~~~~~~~~~~~~~~~~~~

- **September 1994** – Lawsuit against Federal government for wrongful death of Vicki Weaver is settled out of court.

~~~~~~~~~~~~~~~~~~

- **September 1995** – Senate Hearings begin on Federal Siege at Ruby Ridge.

~~~~~~~~~~~~~~~~~~

- **August 21, 1997** – Boundary County brings state murder charges against Kevin Harris and involuntary manslaughter charges against Lon Horiuchi.

- **October 11, 1997** – FBI Agent Michael Kahoe receives 18 months sentence and $4000 fine for destroying an agency document concerning the 1992 shootout at Ruby Ridge.

- **October 23, 1997** – Scientific tests prove that U.S. Marshal Larry Cooper killed Sam Weaver.

- **November 14, 1997** – Murder charges against Kevin Harris are dropped.

~~~~~~~~~~~~~~~~~~~

- **January 8, 1998** – FBI Sniper Lon Horiuchi is ordered to stand trial on the involuntary manslaughter charges.

CHAPTER

3

Life Before Ruby Ridge

Government is like a garden. It needs to be weeded now and then.

--"Grandpa" Harvey Weaver

I was raised near the small town of Villisca in southwest Iowa. My earliest memories were of living in a rented farmhouse about 15 miles north of Villisca and attending kindergarten through fifth grade at Griswold, Iowa.

Surrounded by hard working and conservative farm people, I was raising chickens and selling eggs at age seven. Most of our friends, relatives and neighbors were farmers of German decent and very conservative, politically speaking. My grandfather, Harvey Weaver, had lost his farm during the depression. I remember him saying, "Government is like a garden. It needs to be weeded now and then."

In the early 1950's our evening entertainment was listening to the radio. On many Saturday mornings I would listen to the *Lone Ranger* while I washed the dishes. Mom was a very neat housekeeper, and still is today at the age of 81. She taught us that dishes were to be washed, dried and put away after each meal.

We got our first television in 1954. It was a Coronado® brand. Dad bought it from his brother Cecil who owned the Gambles store in Villisca. One of my favorite programs was *The Big Picture*, a World War II documentary. Watching this and saying the "Pledge of Allegiance" in school every morning gave me a strong sense of patriotism and pride in my country. Stalin was certainly right when he said that television would become the most effective propaganda tool invented. It certainly has been for my generation.

Dad bought me my first BB gun when I was ten. He taught me how to use it and always stressed safety. In a few years I graduated to rifles and shotguns. Dad would take me hunting for birds and other small game. He never carried a weapon himself and I never saw him kill anything in his lifetime. He had a very gentle spirit. Dad passed away in October of 1996 at the age of 88.

In August of 1959 we left the farm and moved to Jefferson, Iowa. Dad switched jobs from selling Chevrolets to selling feed and fertilizer for the Walnut Grove Company. My sisters and I didn't want to move but we quickly made new friends and the adjustment was easy.

Between sixth grade and graduation I worked as a substitute paper carrier for the *Des Moines Register*. I also worked selling shoes, bailing hay and ran a hobby shop. I wrapped meat in a market and shoveled more than my share of snow for friends and neighbors and dined out often.

After seventh grade I didn't care much for school but was able to maintain average grades without having to work at it. I didn't learn to enjoy reading until my early 30's, at which time I began to read everything I could get my hands on. The old saying, "ignorance is bliss" can be so true in certain ways.

Some of the books that I would recommend are: *1984* by George Orwell, *None Dare Call It Conspiracy* by Gary Allen, *The Final Reformation* by C.J. Koster, *Babylon Mystery Religion* by Ralph Woodrow, *Unintended Consequences* by John Ross, *Atlas Shrugged* by Ayn Rand, *101 Things to Do 'Til the Revolution* by Claire Wolfe, and *Called to Serve* by Colonel James "Bo" Gritz.

I attended a small junior college in Fort Dodge, Iowa for two years. To help pay for my schooling, I drove a school bus and loaded pop trucks during the school year. In the summer months I worked on road construction.

It was during my second year of college when I met a beautiful dark haired young woman by the name of Vicki Jean Jordison. We became friends and dated a few times. Then, in October of 1968 I joined the Army and we didn't see each other for a couple of years.

My three-year hitch in the army was fairly uneventful, as I was assigned stateside duty. I am proud that I completed the rigorous Special Forces training and earned my Green Beret. I was assigned to the Seventh Special Forces Group in November of 1969. At the time, I was disappointed that I wasn't going to Viet Nam. Now that I am older and wiser I realize that it was fortunate to have been given stateside duty.

During my third year in the service Vicki and I started dating again. We fell in love, and were married within a month of my discharge from the Army in October of 1971.

Vicki and I were no different from many hard working Americans. We enjoyed the company of friends and neighbors.

After four years of marriage, we had not yet had any children. Vicki wanted to adopt a child and I suggested buying a Chevrolet Corvette instead. We bought the Corvette, only to find out six weeks later that Vicki had become pregnant. Our first child, Sara, was born in the spring of '76. We ended up trading the Corvette in on a family car.

Two years after Sara was born, we had our second child. He was a healthy little boy born in the spring of '78. We named him Samuel Hanson after both of his grandfather's middle names. Sam and Sara became inseparable. Rachel was born in the fall of '81. She was a quiet, happy little baby.

Vicki and I became interested in the study of history, politics, and religion. Apparently, some people were offended as our religious and political views changed. We soon realized that people who seek truth and share what they have learned, are quickly out of the main stream. Those that do share can pay a high price. It could cost them their job, reputation or even their life. Most people are content to go through life believing only what they've been taught at either school or church.

The mind unlearns with difficulty what it has long learned.
    --Seneca

It was during this period that a one-time friend named Woody, contacted the IRS and told them we were trying to solicit others to form a tax protest movement and stop paying taxes. This was a lie! We had always paid our taxes, which was easily confirmed in an IRS audit in 1985. Later, we found out that Woody was in trouble with the IRS and was trying to make himself look good at our expense.

We decided to separate from what we saw as a meaningless existence in suburbia. Our decision to leave Iowa and move west was not an easy one. It took us several years and we still had mixed emotions about it. Quitting your job, leaving family and friends, selling most of what you own to move to a place you have never been, is more risk than most people are willing to take.

Vicki and I had come to the conclusion that we wanted to raise our children away from the rat race and the ever-increasing intrusions of government. I could no longer envision spending the rest of my life working in a factory for forty or fifty hours a week and waiting all year for my three-week vacation. Putting up with ten-hour days behind the wheel on crowded roads, rushing from one tourist trap to another, is not my idea of a vacation anyway.

After we had decided to move west, another so called friend named Shannon, told us about a reporter who wanted to interview us. Our friend assured us that Dan Dunden of the *Waterloo Courier* would be fair and honest. We were receptive to the offer. We saw it as a good chance to share our true beliefs and refute some of the gossip and lies being spread by people like Woody.

During the interview we kept trying to explain our views and philosophies. Dunden indicated to us that he wasn't interested in what we thought. He wanted to talk about survivalists. He wanted to see our food supplies and especially our guns and ammunition. Shannon had evidently told him that survivalists often build fortified compounds with a 300-yard "kill zone" around them. Dunden asked if we were going to do that. We told him no, that we didn't think that sort of thing was necessary.

When the article came out in the paper, Dunden had lied and said we *were* going to build a fortified compound with a 300-yard "kill zone". *(Later, Dunden would repeat this lie in court, under oath. Although he had tape-recorded the interview, Dunden now claims he lost the tape. The Feds then used this 300 yard "kill zone" statement as part of their "psychological profile" to determine how dangerous our family was.)*

Vicki and I were now branded with media fostered lies; that we were tax protesters, and that we were ready to kill people. *(As recent as 1997, in a Readers Digest article, we were described as tax protestors. After five years you would think the Feds could get the facts straight.)*

In the summer of '83 we sold our house, my Harley Davidson, and other possessions we wouldn't need in the mountains. We bought a one-ton moving van and a trailer to pull behind the pickup. The kids were excited. Everything was going smoothly until Sam jumped off the truck and broke his foot the day before we left. We pulled out in mid-August in sweltering heat.

We weren't exactly sure where we were headed, but decided the mountains of the Pacific Northwest would be our final destination. To make the trip less monotonous for the kids we did some sightseeing along the way. We visited such places as *Reptile Gardens*, *Sea World* and the Black Hills area of South Dakota.

Our goal and our dream as we left, was to move into the mountains to be free. Free to worship the Creator in our own way, to build a home and live as self-sufficient as possible. We were not looking to do *battle* with anyone. We did not *hate* anyone. *We wanted to be left alone.*

CHAPTER

Home on the Mountain

Ruby Ridge is a name fabricated by the press, and even though it is incorrect, it is a name that will forever be burned into the memories of many people.

--Sara Weaver

We had decided that northern Idaho would be a good place to look for property. We began searching in the Wallace, Idaho, area and worked our way north. Within three or four weeks we found the property we liked approximately eight miles south of Bonners Ferry. It is now known as Ruby Ridge.

We would like to set the record straight as far as the term "Ruby Ridge" is concerned. There really is no Ruby Ridge, at least not where our property is located. The real name is Caribou Ridge and Ruby Creek Drainage. Ruby Ridge is a name fabricated by the press, and even though it is incorrect, it is a name that will forever be burned into the memories of many people.

We had $5,000 cash and a one-ton moving van that we used to purchase 20 acres of land that consisted mostly of trees and rocks. There are hills and steep ravines, but not much level land. One of the prettiest areas of the property is the knoll. It's kind of a round hump on the side of a higher mountain and the ground recedes sharply from all sides. This is where Vicki and I decided to build our home. It is kind of difficult to get to, but the view is well worth the effort.

The driveway to the knoll is on the northwest side. Also to the northwest is a view of "Old Roman Nose", a large mountain that was burned off in a forest fire and has a ridge that resembles a nose. Directly to the west is another large mountain with trees as thick as "Old Roman Nose" is naked. To the north is a smaller mountain that is partially treed and has lots of rugged looking rocks. The south overlooks a large beautiful valley, as does the east. The view from all sides is absolutely breathtaking.

There is also a spring we used for water that has never quit running, even through dry summers and cold winters. The water is just a trickle, but it is clean, pure, and dependable.

We started building our cabin in the fall of 1983. At the time we were renting a trailer from Arthur Briggs. The trailer was located in the meadow about a mile below our property. In the mornings Vicki would put on a stew or roast for lunch. She and I would head up the mountain to work on the cabin while the kids stayed below and played with the neighbors' children. When we returned in the evening, our dinner consisted of leftovers from lunch.

By the time the cabin shell was completed we were running out of money. Vicki said we should sell her diamond ring to help pay for the roof. I was against the idea but she was pretty persuasive.

The house sat on the northeast corner of the knoll. On the left side of the front of the house sat a huge rock. At the highest point it stands approximately six feet and is nearly as long as a pickup. It butted lengthwise right up to the side of our front porch. There was a rock path that sprawled out in front of the porch and led to our root cellar.

Directly north of where the house sat (the unoccupied house collapsed under heavy snow in the spring of 1997 and is no longer there) is a steep ravine that drops down into a birch grove. This grove edges the lower part of our driveway, which is fairly flat until it reaches the base of the knoll. Here it takes a steep incline. To the left of this incline is a large outcropping of rocks, which served as a viewpoint on the outskirts of the knoll.

From these rocks we could see most of our driveway which enabled us to spot anyone approaching long before they reached the front door. We could also hear a vehicle slowly creeping up the steep mountain road long before they made it to our drive. It was always exciting for the kids to anticipate who might be coming to visit, and they would run out to the rock outcropping to find out who it was as soon as possible.

On the east side of the knoll is a cliff. On the edge of the cliff sits a huge boulder. It appears to be perched there, barely hanging on. It's a bit of a thrill to step down onto that rock overlooking the valley. You get the feeling that your weight could easily shake the boulder loose and send you plunging to the earth far below.

Our home was very comfortable. There were three bedrooms, all on the second floor. Downstairs there was a livingroom, bathroom, kitchen, and a pantry. Vicki also had a sewing corner where she created some very useful and aesthetic things. Our kitchen contained both a wood burning cookstove and a propane stove, a fair amount of counter space and shelves full of herbs and spices.

Vicki did a lot to make our home comfortable. She varnished the cabinets and the floors, made all the curtains, as well as cushions for the furniture. She made quilts for the beds and rugs for the floor. Blue was her favorite color and it was a color reflected in most of what she did. The house stayed cozy and warm through the coldest of winters thanks to the good insulation and our airtight woodstove in the livingroom. It held coals all night long and started right up in the morning.

Other buildings on our property included a chicken house, an outhouse, a woodshed, a pump house and a root cellar.

It was during this time that we met Kevin Harris. Kevin was 16 years old and his mom had sent him to live with an ex-boyfriend of hers named Phil. Phil had come up with a novel idea to raise money for a down payment on the land he was living on. He was cutting and selling firewood off of the property. Kevin worked like a slave and had to live on squash and tomatoes, which was about all Phil would give him to eat.

It wasn't long before Kevin began spending time with our family. He couldn't get enough of Vicki's home cooking. When he wasn't working for Phil he would help us work on the cabin. Other times he would be off fishing with Sara and Sam.

Kevin was disappointed that fall when Phil decided to send him back home to Spokane. Our family had grown close to Kevin and I told him if he ever wanted to move back to Idaho that he was welcome to stay with us. He was back within two weeks. He stayed with us off and on over the next nine years.

I had originally planned to build the cabin below our spring so we could have gravity fed water year round. Vicki insisted we build on top of the knoll to have full advantage of the view. My father-in-law, Dave, helped us improve the property in many ways. He helped me build a system whereby we could pump water from the spring into two large barrels outside the house. At least we had gravity fed water in the summer months.

20

We couldn't bury the water line because of the rocky ground. In the winter the line would freeze so we had to haul water. Sam trained his dog Striker, a yellow Lab, to pull containers of water on a sled using a harness he and Sara made. Striker was like a draft horse. After a few trips he knew the routine and was eager to work.

I bought two horses. Amigo was half-Arabian and half-Belgian. I used him to skid logs. Sara's horse was a gray dapple Arabian appropriately named Lightning. Sara began riding her horse bareback at age seven. To this day horses are one of her favorite hobbies.

We raised chickens for eggs and butchering. Rachel enjoyed taking care of them. In fact, she had a Barred Rock hen named Rocky that adored her and followed her around like a dog. The kids enjoyed the companionship of all the animals.

The first few years on the ridge were everything we could have hoped for. It seemed to be the ideal life. We worked hard but we were working for ourselves. We came together as a family in a way that probably would not have been possible in the nine-to-five world of city life. There were sacrifices. We may have been lacking in money and luxuries but we were rewarded in other ways. We became more self-reliant and self-sufficient. We learned to depend on each other.

Vicki home schooled our children. She had earned an Associates Degree in education. Her classroom routine usually consisted of four hours study per day, four days per week. Sara proved to be an excellent student but Sam was less enthused. Like a lot of boys, he wanted to be outside, preferably fishing. Sam finally caught on and became an avid reader. One of Sam's favorite subjects was history. He was soon quoting out of the Scriptures, the encyclopedia and knew our Constitution verbatim. I had never seen Vicki happier than she was in those first few years on the mountain. This was her calling.

Vicki was a petite and beautiful woman of Scotch and English descent. She had dark brown eyes and dark brown hair that had a red tint in the sunlight. Her smile lit up her face. In addition to her good looks and charm she could do anything. She ran her home, took care of the kids and found the time to make some of our clothes. She exemplified everything that a wife and mother should be. A perfectionist, she never left a job unfinished.

Vicki had a passion for refinishing old furniture. She loved to strip away the old finish and expose the natural wood grain. After sanding and repairing as needed, she would stain and varnish. When she was finished the piece looked as new. She was great at making something out of nothing. She could also stretch twenty dollars further than anyone I've known.

I have fond memories of Vicki teaching Sara how to make rugs. They took old sweatshirts and rolled them into balls, sorted by color. When they had enough they would string a wooden two by four loom with yarn and weave the fabric into a rug. It took about five hours to make one. Sara was sure proud when her mother sold some of the rugs for extra cash.

When Sam wasn't reading or busy with his chores, he was after his big sister to go fishing with him. They would spend hours fishing and exploring. Most of the time they brought home enough brook trout for supper. Sam and Sara were very close and did almost everything together.

Rachel was still pretty young and spent most of her time "helping" her mother in the house or garden. Her help often made a chore take longer but Vicki was very patient and never scolded her for it.

One afternoon, on our anniversary, I took Vicki down to the Deep Creek Inn for coffee. We left the kids at home with Sara in charge. While we were gone the kids came up with the idea to bake us a cake. Sam chopped the kindling and got the wood stove going. While Rachel cleaned the house, Sara made a chocolate cake from scratch. We learned later that the hard part was trying to spell "anniversary". Sam saved the day when he found it in the dictionary. The cake wasn't perfect but Vicki and I were never so pleased and proud of our children, as we were that night over dessert with them.

In addition to their school lessons, we worked hard teaching the children values. We stressed respect and appreciation for each other, and above all, honesty. Like all kids, ours had their share of fights and arguments. They always worked out their differences, and disputes were quickly forgotten. We were always proud of our kids. They were not mean spirited and they never talked back to us. My kids are my pride and joy.

5

The Setup

No one is bound to obey an unconstitutional law and no courts are bound to enforce it.

--16 Am. Jur., Sec. 177 late 2d, Sec. 256

Taking my gun away because I might shoot someone is like cutting my tongue out just because I might yell, "Fire!" in a crowded theater.

--Peter Venetoklis

A "snitch" is usually someone, who has committed a crime, but when apprehended is given a chance to avoid arrest or prosecution by agreeing to become an informant. Whether a first time offender, or someone with an extensive criminal history, these people are essentially put on the payroll (your tax dollars at work). They work as undercover informants, in theory, providing the controlling agency with information on crimes and criminals.

The problem, in most cases, is the informant's prime motivations: money and staying out of jail. Informants are pressured to produce, to provide information that will lead to arrest and ultimately enhance the agency's image. Many times, the information is invalid or an outright lie. The potential for abuse is great. In the past few years an alarming number of innocent people have been killed or imprisoned by overly zealous law enforcement officers acting on bad tips provided by snitches.

--Randy Weaver

I met Frank K. in 1984. Frank was a bit on the goofy side, always talking about ways to get even with the government. In retrospect I wondered many times if he wasn't a snitch. It was Frank who talked me into attending my first Aryan Nation World Congress near Hayden Lake, Idaho in '86. He suggested we go down and "see what it's all about." At the time I was not aware of the magnitude of the governments efforts to infiltrate right wing organizations.

I already knew that I didn't agree with the supremacist philosophy held by the Aryan Nation members, but I was curious and I'm always interested in learning more about religious beliefs. Frank and I drove down to hear what they had to say.

There was quite an assortment of people there from all over the U.S., a few from Europe and some from Canada. I talked to a number of people there who also did not agree with the Aryan Nation racial views. They, like me, enjoyed sharing common beliefs and learning about different viewpoints.

I only listened to a couple of the scheduled speakers in their church before I realized I didn't want to hear any more tirades against non-whites. I was much more comfortable outside at the picnic tables mingling with the crowd. I can understand hating someone because they hurt you or your family, but to hate someone just because they're of another race, is sheer ignorance.

It was at this '86 congress that Frank introduced me to Gus Magisono. I don't know if Frank knew him from before or had just met him. Gus was dressed like a biker and introduced himself as a gunrunner. He said he was raised a Catholic but didn't know what he believed now. I think a person should know what they believe and why. Gus didn't appear very bright and I didn't spend a lot of time talking to him.

The following year I ran into him at the '87 World Congress. He indicated that his gun running business was going well and we spent some time talking. I could only take being around Frank and Gus for so long. Frank liked to talk about big deals that required money and brains to pull off. He had neither. When the two of them got together they would ramble on about robbing armories and stealing machine guns. This is where I would usually walk away.

Frank contacted me in the winter of '87 and said that Gus wanted to meet us in Sandpoint, Idaho. I'd been on the mountain awhile so I agreed to go. When we arrived, Gus got in the car with us. Frank, the big shot, pulled out a carpenters stud finder and proceeded to "check" Gus for electronic bugs! I thought to myself, "What an idiot!" I found out during the trial that he had been wired that day. So much for the stud finder.

Gus and Frank were soon talking about starting up a militant group and blowing up dams. Gus wanted to know about the "patriot movement" and how we could "start" one. I let them do most of the talking. After a while I told them I needed to head for home, so Frank and I left.

I skipped the '88 Congress but went back in '89 with Vicki and the kids. It is beautiful country around Hayden Lake, Idaho and a weekend getaway was a welcome break. I saw Gus again and we talked for awhile. He said he needed more guns for his clients and indicated that I could make a lot of money with him. I told him I wasn't interested, but if he was ever in our neighborhood to look us up.

Several months later, in the fall of '89, he showed up at our house with Frank. I was fed up with Frank and his line of bull and told him to leave. Gus wanted to know if I knew Chuck. H., an old Klansman who was living in Montana. I had met Chuck at Hayden Lake and he seemed to be pretty tight with Rev. Butler, who runs the church there.

Gus asked me if I would take him to Montana and make an introduction. We talked about other things but he kept coming back to Chuck. I told him we might be able to go in a few weeks. I have since learned that Gus supposedly had information that Chuck was going to start up a KKK group in Noxon, Montana.

During the U.S. Senate hearings concerning Ruby Ridge, Senator Arlen Spectre asked Gus how I fit into all of this. He replied, "I was going to use Weaver simply as an introductory tool."

Gus called me in October of '89 and we met at a restaurant in Bonners Ferry. He still wanted to know when we could make the trip to Montana and asked if I knew where he could get any guns. We talked about which weapons he thought were "in demand" and he said he needed some sawed-off shotguns.

Winter was on the way and Vicki and I were broke. We had been renting a house by the highway for the past year and a half and couldn't afford to pay any more rent. We planned to move back to the cabin on the mountain. Against my better judgement, I told Gus I had a couple of shotguns I could sell, a Remington 870 pump and a single shot.

When I asked him what I could get for them he said, "Sawed-off, I'll give you $700 for both." He was lying and only paid $400 total in two payments. I wondered why he didn't cut the barrels himself. I showed him my 870-pump shotgun and asked him where he wanted it cut. He pointed to the barrel by the end of the magazine tube. Several days later he called and asked if I was going to do "that job" we had talked about, and I said I would do it. The Feds had taped this conversation.

I met Gus in Sandpoint on the 24th of October. We drove to the park along the lake and I gave the guns to him. He complimented me on the fine job I had done. Then he told me he could only pay $450 for them and only had $300 of that.

I needed the money and agreed to the deal. He said he would pay me the balance when we went to Montana. We agreed to meet again the following month.

Not long after this, Rico V. (whom I later found out was an FBI snitch) told me "stay away from Gus, he's dirty." I said, "Oh great!" I didn't tell him I had already sold guns to Gus. I assume Rico must have revealed this to me because he wanted to gain my confidence so that he could move in on Gus and pull a sting operation on me.

The last time I met with Gus was in November of '89 at which time I asked him for the $150 he owed me. He only had $100 so I took it. I confronted him about being a snitch. He started swearing and vehemently denied it. I told him to forget Montana because I wasn't going with him. Then I left and didn't see him again until my trial in '93.

Approximately six months after that last meeting with Gus, the head of the ATF in Spokane, Washington, Herb B. told me that I would be charged with six or seven federal firearms violations if I didn't go undercover and work with him. He had cornered Vicki and I at a friend's home, and was driving a U.S. Forest Service vehicle. I laughed and told him, "Forget it." Earlier that same day, Herb had posed as a Forest Service agent to my children, and lied to them claiming he was looking for a man lost in the area.

Another six months passed before they arrested my wife and I on Ruby Creek Road in a ruse where a man and woman were pretending to be in need of help with a broken down pickup and camper. They used this plan because they knew that Vicki and I had big hearts and would stop to help anyone that had broken down on the road. When I stepped up to the truck to look at the engine compartment, the man standing there grabbed the front of my jacket, stuck a 9MM pistol in my face and said, "Freeze, Randy, you're under arrest!" He started yelling, "Get down! Get

29

down! Get down!" which I immediately did. Although I couldn't see it, the female agent was throwing Vicki face down into the mud and snow also. Five or six other agents had been hiding in the camper and another agent with a sniper rifle had been hiding in the woods in white camouflage. Later, the same ATF agent who had stuck the gun in my face, and his boss, claimed I had resisted arrest. I didn't have a chance to resist, even if I had wanted to. His boss, Herb B., also told the U.S. Marshals that I had been a suspect in bank holdups in Montana. That was entirely false information. Vicki asked the agents to see a copy of the arrest warrant; they told her she could see it later.

Approximately 20 minutes after our arrest, Vicki was released and I was taken to the county jail in Coeur d'Alene, Idaho. I was released the following day after signing my property over as a promissory bond to assure my appearance in court on February 19, 1990. The magistrate told me that I would lose my property if I lost my case in court. This led us to believe that we would most likely lose our property; I'd be sitting in prison and Vicki and the kids would be homeless. *(The magistrate later admitted, during the trial in Boise, that he had given us erroneous information about the property bond.)*

Within a week or so, my probation officer sent me a letter stating that the court date was to be March 20, 1990, when in fact it had been changed to *February 20, 1990.* When I didn't show up for court on the February 20th date, it was broadcast over the radio that I was like a "wild animal" up in the mountains, but that the U.S. Marshals would "bring me in". When I sent a copy of the document stating the March 20, 1990, court date to the media, they confronted the U.S. Marshals' office in Boise. The Marshals' office lied and denied that it had happened. It was at that point that we decided to stay on the mountain. We hoped that there was someone who cared enough to seek out the truth and help us get through this whole mess. I guess you could say we were looking for a miracle.

The ATF had lied to us on numerous occasions. Then they lied to the U.S. Marshals Service when they took over the case after I failed to appear in court. I assume they wanted to create a heightened or exaggerated profile of me so that the marshals would pursue me more aggressively. I also believe that a big part for the exaggeration was that I had apparently "bruised" Herb B.'s ego. After the deadly shootout on August 21, 1992, the U.S. Marshals further exaggerated the profile and lied like hell when the case was turned over to the FBI. I believe that is why they came after us in such a terrorist fashion. The FBI, in turn, lied to the entire world and continues to do so to this day.

CHAPTER

6

Praying for a Miracle

Truth is only philosophical.

--Dave Hunt, U.S. Marshal

If I believed that 'Truth is only philosophical' I'll come off the mountain and be the best damned snitch you've ever had.

--Randy Weaver

After February 22, 1991, we had resolved to stay home in an act of what could be considered "civil disobedience". Various government agencies had lied to us and deceived us so many times that we felt totally betrayed. We believed that no citizen of this country should be treated in the manner in which we were being treated.

Although I had been entrapped on the gun charge, we knew I was facing serious prison time with only a public defender to represent me. Also, because of erroneous information given to us by a federal magistrate we believed that our home and property would be confiscated. That would leave me in jail, and Vicki and the kids on the street.

We were just trying to keep our family together the only way we knew how. For eighteen months we were basically praying for a miracle.

During that time many friends and relatives came to visit bringing supplies, advice and moral support. Sometimes these folks would bring messages from the U.S. Marshals who were watching us. Since August 1992 we have figured out that we were also hosts to several snitches and federal agents who were lying and deceiving us. They would sit in our home and "chat", as Vicki served them coffee and cookies.

Not once during the whole fiasco did the local sheriff have the courage to do his job. He never made the effort to come to our house and knock on the door to try and figure out what was going on. He instead decided to cower to the intimidation of the Feds. In fact, during our trial, it was alluded to that the U.S. Marshal's Service had bribed him with money. *"Surely, there is nothing new under the sun."*

One beautiful event that occurred during the eighteen-month stay on the mountain before the siege, was the arrival of our youngest child, Elisheba Anne. Vicki gave birth to her in October of '91. Despite thirty-six hours of hard labor, she said having me help her deliver the child at home was a more joyous experience than delivering in a hospital. Vicki was so tiny, yet so tough!

To this day, the U.S. Marshals claim they did their best to negotiate with us. These are empty words to say the least. They don't have the legal authority to negotiate. I however tried to accommodate them when they would ask me what it would take to bring about my surrender. Two or three times I sent my surrender terms to them. I said that I wanted my .22 caliber pistol back, (which they had taken from me during my initial arrest on Ruby Creek Road) and I asked that the ATF admit that I had been entrapped on the gun charge. I also wanted the local sheriff to apologize for calling me "paranoid" and "dangerous" in a report to the U.S. Marshall's Service.

Actually, I think U.S. Marshall Dave Hunt was just playing a waiting game. I believe he was hoping that I would tire of staying home on the mountain, and short of that, maybe I would wander into the woods far enough that a SWAT team could ambush me. The latter is basically what eventually happened.

Totally frustrated, I sent a message to Dave Hunt stating that all I wanted was **the truth**. He replied, "Truth is only philosophical." My final message to him was, "If I believed that 'Truth is only philosophical' , I'll come off the mountain and be the best damned snitch you've ever had."

Needless to say, the miracle we needed never arrived.

7

The Siege

By Randy Weaver

*Government is not reason, it is not eloquence; it is force.
Like fire, it is a dangerous servant and a fearful master.*

--George Washington

The date was August 21, 1992. About 10:30 that morning, Striker, our yellow Labrador Retriever, was down by the pump house. He began barking excitedly. This had happened off and on during the 18 months we were secluded on the mountain, but this time was different. The dog seemed more excited than usual.

Normally, I would not have followed the dog, nor allowed the boys to follow him into the woods. This time, however, Sam and Kevin followed Striker while I walked down an old logging road that paralleled their direction. After several hundred feet, the old road intersected with another one. This intersection later became known as the "Y".

I was just about in the center of this intersection when an armed man dressed in exceptionally good cammo jumped out and said, "Freeze, Randy!" I yelled back, "Fuck you!" and retreated back up the logging road toward home.

I was about 430 feet from the "Y" when I heard a gunshot and Striker start yelping. Shortly afterward, I heard two more shots and Striker was silent. I yelled to the boys, **"Get home, they've shot the dog, get home!"** I heard more shots and guessed that someone was shooting at Sam and Kevin.

Hoping to draw attention away from the boys, I fired a shot straight into the air with my double barrel shotgun. The shooting continued. I was so scared that when I tried to reload my shotgun I shoved the shell past the extractor jamming the gun. I could neither close the weapon nor remove the shell with my fingers. Still yelling for the boys to get home, I fired three shots into the air with my 9-mm pistol. Finally, Sam yelled, "I'm coming Dad!" Feeling relieved, I quickly headed for home.

The relief was short-lived when a few minutes later Kevin came walking up the driveway, crying. We all yelled, "Where's Sam?" Kevin replied, "Sam's dead." I lost control of my emotions and started crying, cussing and praying all at the same time.

Vicki had been wearing a skirt so she ran back to the house to put jeans on. When she returned she said, "We have to get Sam." Kevin said Sam's body was lying in the middle of the road just up from the "Y". I believed we would surely be shot, but at that moment, I didn't care.

(We found out later that the men who killed Sam were still there, hiding in the woods watching us retrieve his body. It's obvious they knew they had killed him. For some reason they decided not to take our lives at that time.)

We carried Sam's body home and placed him in a small guest shed. Shortly after, we began hearing all kinds of sirens in the valley below us. Needless to say, we were in a state of shock and sadness. We sat around the house not knowing what to expect next.

We heard on a radio news broadcast that we had supposedly ambushed some U.S. Marshals, murdering one of them. Kevin said that he thought he might have hit one of them, but only fired his rifle in self-defense after the marshals began shooting at Sam. There was no further contact with anyone through the night and most of the next day.

It was about 4:30 p.m. that next day when the two dogs still tied in the yard began to whimper and bark. I said I would go out and check on the dogs and see if anyone was out there who might want to talk to us. Sara and Kevin went with me and we walked out to the rock outcropping that overlooked the driveway. The dogs had settled down and everything seemed peaceful now. No one showed themselves or said anything, so I assumed there was no one there. I decided to walk over to the guest shed to be with Sam one more time. This proved to be a big mistake.

As I reached up to unlatch the door, someone shot me in the back. A bloody mist smelling like fresh hamburger crossed my face, accompanied by a loud bang and a very sharp pain. It felt like I had been kicked in the shoulder by a mule. I thought that whoever fired the shot was standing behind me, not more than ten feet away. Believing I was going to be shot again, I turned around to spit in the coward's face. There was no one there.

At this same moment, Sara came up behind me and asked what had happened. I said, "I've been shot." She said, "Get to the house! Get to the house!" and started shoving me in that direction. Vicki stepped outside with Elisheba in her arms and yelled, "What happened?" I said,

"I've been shot Ma!" Totally out of character, Vicki swore as loud as she could' "You bastards!" and told us to get into the house.

Vicki was still holding Elisheba in one arm and holding the door open for us with the other. I heard another loud bang and a commotion behind me as I went through the doorway first, followed by Sara and Kevin. When I turned around I saw Kevin lying on his back, just inside the doorway. Vicki was on her knees with her head resting on the floor. Ten-month-old Elisheba was beneath her.

Sara and Rachel immediately began screaming and crying. Their mother had just been shot through the head and killed. The same bullet had struck Kevin, wounding him seriously. Elisheba had her mother's blood and bone fragments in her hair and on her clothing but was unharmed physically. I picked her up from beneath Vicki and handed her to Rachel.

After I got Vicki's body into the kitchen, we covered her with a blanket and turned our attention to Kevin. I told him we needed to get a tourniquet on his arm but he said, "Don't worry about it. Just let me die, it hurts like hell." After a short while, Kevin said, "Help me up Weaver, I'm not dying." (We found out later that the bullet passed through his upper left arm, broke two ribs and lodged near his heart.)

Later that night the pain was so bad that Kevin asked me to kill him by shooting him in the head when he wasn't looking. I told him I couldn't do it, he would have to use his good arm and do it himself. My daughters started crying and pleading with Kevin, begging him not to do it. They said, "We've lost too many already." Thankfully, Kevin is still with us today.

We listened to the radio station out of Bonners Ferry on our battery-operated radio. Throughout the siege we would tune in only to hear the false reports given to the media by the federal agencies. These reports, so full of lies and errors, reinforced our feelings of total helplessness, anger, frustration and deep sorrow.

Striker had been killed, shot up the rear as he was running toward home. Sam was dead, shot in the back while running home. I had been shot from behind while

40

trying to check on Sam's body in the shed. Vicki had been shot and killed standing in the doorway of her home while holding our infant daughter in her arms. The same bullet that killed Vicki had seriously wounded Kevin. At this point, I truly believed they intended to kill all of us. How does a father explain to his children, who have already lost their mother and brother, that in all likelihood they too would be killed? I couldn't understand it myself.

Sunday, I could hear some type of motorized vehicle that sounded like a military tank driving around the yard. Apparently they were smashing outbuildings and anything else that got in the way. I later found out that it was an armored personnel carrier. The thought crossed my mind that they would destroy the guest shed where Sam's body was laying. I wanted to run out to stop them, but I knew that would be an act of suicide. Later we heard a news report on the radio that stated they had taken Sam's body out of the shed. It was also reported that Kevin or I had probably shot him!

Sam's grandparents, Dave and Jean Jordison, arrived from Iowa on Sunday, August 23, 1992. They were kept under constant surveillance during the entire standoff. They found out about Sam's death on the national news on Monday, August 24, 1992. The Federal agents who were watching them didn't have the courage or decency to tell them in person.

Dave and Jean, as well as many other friends and relatives, offered to come and talk to us but they all were told that it was too dangerous and we might take them hostage. I believe that the real reason the Feds did not want anyone talking to us is that they realized they had screwed up and didn't want the truth to get out.

There were many protestors from all over the country who had gathered at the police roadblock two miles from home. Their presence put the Federal agents in a quandary as to what to do next. I believe this slowed their actions down and bought us the time that we desperately needed.

Former Green Beret, Colonel James "Bo" Gritz and Jack McLamb, a former Phoenix police officer, were eventually successful in convincing the FBI agent in charge to allow them to come up and speak to us. After our initial meeting with Gritz on August 28, 1992, the FBI finally had to admit they had killed Vicki. Probably the biggest determinant in convincing us to surrender was the fact that the famous defense attorney, Gerry Spence, introduced through Gritz, had promised to look into the case and defend us if he felt that we were innocent.

Kevin left the cabin and surrendered on August 30, 1992. The girls and I came out the following day.

Shortly thereafter, Sam and Vicki's bodies were cremated, but not until after the FBI had snipped Vicki's fingers off and sent them to the FBI laboratory in Quantico, VA. Her fingers were never returned for cremation. When questioned about it no one seemed to have an answer as to what they did with them.

CHAPTER

8

Memories of Despair

By Sara Weaver

Liberty! O Liberty! What crimes are committed in thy name!

--Mme. Roland,
On her way to the guillotine

What Are You Going To Do?

By Sara Weaver

Where are we all headed?
I call it the yellow brick road to hell.
Jesters prowl the alleyways,
Looking for souls to sell.

Demons adorned with glowing eyes
Hunt you in the night.
Your thoughts are scattered in the wind,
There is only room for fright.

They have stolen your souls, and held you in chains
Feasting upon your fear.
They never fail to remind you,
The Grim Reaper is always near.

There is no one to stop the madness
Except one – and that is you.
Will your fear let them continue the game?
What are you going to do?

This chapter is an account of the siege on our family in August of 1992 as I remember it happening. I struggle to this day trying to understand it all. I know I will probably never know (in this life anyway) why it happened to our family, but I hope and pray it never happens to anyone else.

This account is brutal and honest. You the reader may find it disturbing and graphic. Sadly enough, real life tragic events usually are.

Friday, August 21, 1992

I woke up to what seemed to be a normal morning. There was no premonition, no warning of what was coming. Other than the dogs acting a little restless, everything was quiet. We figured it was probably the scent of a deer or bear bothering them. At about 10:30 a.m., something set the dogs off and they began barking. Dad, Kevin and Sam picked up their weapons and headed out to the rock that over-looked our driveway. Striker, our yellow Lab, was racing in that direction barking frantically. Sam yelled back towards the house that he thought he had heard something in the woods, and that he was going to follow Striker.

The three of them started down the drive following the dog. I walked out to the rock to wait for them, and watched as they disappeared into the woods at the end of our driveway. I figured they would soon chase off whatever animal it was. Five minutes or so had passed when a gunshot made me jump. My heart dropped straight to my stomach. Dad never shot game in the summer months.

I heard two more shots and then my dad started yelling. At first I couldn't make out the words. Then, **"THEY SHOT STRIKER! SAM! KEVIN! THEY SHOT STRIKER!!"** The whole time my dad was yelling I heard more gunfire. I couldn't think, I couldn't breath. *Please let them be okay. Who shot Striker? Who keeps shooting? Why would anyone shoot Striker?* All of this raced through my mind as I forced my legs to move, and ran for the house.

Mom and Rachel had been on the back porch watching Elisheba as she played with baby toys in her playpen. "Mom! Somebody shot Striker!" Mom picked up Elisheba and followed Rachel and I out to the rock. I grabbed my .22 pistol on the way. When we reached the rock, we waited for a few minutes, dumbstruck, before we saw Dad walking up the drive. We all began fearfully asking what had happened and where were Kevin and Sam?

Dad was crying, "I don't know, I don't know, my shotgun jammed." We started begging Dad to hurry and get up the driveway and into the protection of the rocks before some unseen person shot him like they had Striker. We then started yelling for Sam and Kevin, but to no avail. We all were crying and Dad kept saying over and over "My sons, my sons." He was blaming himself for whatever had happened because he had split up from Sam and Kevin when they were following the dog. *(I don't blame my dad for what happened. I never have, and I never will. The events that took place were beyond his control. I pray he will someday stop blaming himself and find peace.)*

Dad went back to the house for another weapon, as his shotgun was useless. While he was gone, Mom, Rachel and I kept yelling Sam and Kevin's names. We heard nothing but our own echoes mocking us, and after the echoes faded, silence.

Dad rejoined us and asked if the boys where back yet. I think he took one look at us and already knew the answer. He started to yell in helplessness, frustration and grief. Dad then took my rifle and fired an entire clip into the air. He said it was to let the neighbors that lived below us know that something was going on. It was about that time that we heard Kevin yell. He was crying, and his hat was missing.

We asked him if he had seen Sam. He said, "Yes, Sam's dead." We all started to sob. Mom was saying **"Are you sure? Are you sure? He can't be dead! He can't be!"** Kevin said, "He's dead. I checked his pulse, there wasn't any. His eyes were open and his face was turning blue."

I felt as though I had been punched in the stomach. I wanted to scream, cry and throw up all at once. My baby brother....**NO!** It wasn't true. It couldn't be. This was all

48

just a horrible nightmare. I was going to wake up any second now. This is the part where you are supposed to wake up! *Please let me wake up!*

I had to do something to keep from going crazy so I began to load the clip that Dad had emptied into the air. It really hadn't hit me yet, that my little brother was dead. **Dead.** How I hate that word. The finality of it. There is no coming back from it. No turning back the clock. No chance for me to stand in his place.

After a few of the worst minutes I had ever experienced in my whole life (or any of our lives for that matter) we all walked back to the house. The afternoon had become unbearably cold, and I don't think it had anything to do with the weather.

I changed from the shorts I had put on that morning to camo pants and a long sleeve shirt. Mom went upstairs to change from her skirt and sandals, into jeans and boots.

When she came back down, she stated matter of factly: "We are going to go and get Sam." I begged her not too. I thought that if they went to get Sam, they would get ambushed and shot as well. Mom and Dad said that they didn't give a damn if they were shot at, they weren't going to just leave him lying in the road.

I think Mom was hoping, no, *believing* that Sam was still alive. Rachel and I took Elisheba and followed them as far as the rock. Mom and Dad started down the driveway first, and Kevin was right behind them. Dad left his rifle at home so he could carry Sam.

A few minutes after they had disappeared from sight, I heard Mom and Dad start to sob and wail, and that was when I knew. This wasn't a dream, and Kevin had not been mistaken.

I waited tensely, fully expecting to hear more gunfire, but all I could hear was my parents sobbing. After a few terribly long minutes, I saw Mom walking up the drive. Dad and Kevin followed carrying Sam's body. That was the last time I saw my little brother. After that first glance I couldn't make myself look at him again. I tried to remember the last time I told him I loved him. I hope he knew. Rather, I hope he knows.

Mom sent me into the guest shed to put a plastic mattress cover on the bed, which I did. Then, I rejoined Rachel and Elisheba at the rock. After they laid Sam's body on the bed, Mom and Dad spent some time cleaning the blood off of him and wrapping him in a sheet. Dad asked if I wanted to see him one last time, but I couldn't do it. That wasn't my Sam in there, the one I had known and loved. That wasn't him shot in the back, his little elbow blown away. No, I couldn't bring myself to enter that shed.

When they were finished, Dad came out carrying Sam's rifle and pistol. He had blood all over his jeans and T-shirt. Like he had just finished cleaning a deer, or butchering chickens. But this, this was Sam's blood, and I had never felt so broken and beaten and totally *heartsick* in all of my life.

Dad showed us Sam's rifle, a .223 caliber. On the rifle's stock, there was a chip of wood missing about a half of an inch long. It seemed that while Sam was running back up the road towards home with his rifle under his arm, a bullet fired from behind him had hit the butt plate of the rifle's stock, putting a dent in it. The bullet then knocked the wood chip off and struck Sam's right elbow nearly cutting his arm off. A second bullet hit him in the middle of his back and exited from his chest. What kind of cowardly bastard does it take to shoot down a fourteen-year-old, eighty pound, adolescent little boy *running away?*

All of us, stunned, shocked and crying had the same question in our minds. *What now? What comes next?* Surely, the people who murdered my brother knew they had screwed up. Wouldn't they now try to verbally make contact with us?

To be on the safe side, we prepared for the worst. We carried food, blankets and ammunition out to the rock. Mom and Kevin filled some water jugs, and then we all went out to the rock to wait, for *what* we didn't know. We sat there for what seemed like forever. And we cried.

After a while, it started to rain. Mom said that it was getting late and that we should all go in. She didn't want Elisheba to catch a cold. We all agreed with her and decided that they would probably try to contact us in the morning somehow, and that it wouldn't do any good to stay outside all night.

Before we went in, Dad and I tied my little dog Buddy, to a tree out behind the chicken coop. From there, he could warn us if someone was trying to sneak up on the house from the south side of the hill. We could hear police sirens in the valley, and traffic on the meadow below.

Whenever Dad went out into the yard to feed the dogs or whatever, I went with him. Not that I could really do anything if something were to happen, but it made me feel better to be with him.

When Dad and I reached the house, Elisheba was napping, and Mom was doing dishes. I told her not to bother with them, and that I would do them for her, but she said she needed to do something to keep from going crazy.

Dad and Kevin brought some food up from the root cellar, but no one felt like eating.

Soon, it was dark. Mom had finished in the kitchen, and had gone upstairs to be alone in her room. We were all sitting around waiting. Waiting and thinking. None of us could stop crying.

Dad got up from his chair and told us he was going out to say goodnight to Sam. He came back a few minutes later and then went upstairs to be with Mom. I had never seen him look so old and beaten.

Rachel and I chose to sleep downstairs that night, instead of upstairs in our room as usual. I don't think either one of us could face the fact that Sam's room was empty.

The long horrible night crept on like a never-ending nightmare for me. Sleep wasn't an option. All night my mind seemed to be stuck on instant replay. I kept thinking about how Sam and I used to do everything together. He and I were pals and best friends; he couldn't *really* be gone. Over and over my mind cruelly replayed the horrible day. *Nothing could be worse than this.* I thought to myself. Little did I know, but the next day was.

Saturday, August 22, 1992

The morning was chilly and foggy. We could still hear more traffic than normal moving about the meadow below. There were helicopters flying around the mountains mostly staying out of sight. We were still waiting.

Dad and Kevin stepped out to feed the dogs and move them out of the rain. Rachel and I made a dash to the outhouse and back. Mom came downstairs and collapsed on the couch sobbing and saying she couldn't believe Sam was dead. We all tried to comfort her but we were soon crying too.

About noon, Dad and I went out to feed the chickens and gather eggs. Mom suggested we try to catch rainwater dripping off the roof just in case we needed extra water, so we moved some five-gallon buckets under the eaves of the porch. After that we just sat around some more, numb with heartache.

Dad and Kevin talked about getting more food from the cellar and changing a propane tank. They never got the chance.

Late in the afternoon the weather started to clear. All was quiet until the dogs started to bark. Dad, Kevin and I picked up our rifles and slipped outside to see what was upsetting them.

By the time we reached the rock, the dogs had quit barking. We stood in the shelter of the rocks for a few minutes. There was no sound or movement of any kind. Everything was calm and quiet. I turned and saw Dad, about fifty feet away, walking towards the shed where Sam had been placed. Dad was on the north side of the shed, the side that faced the mountain. I felt that I should be with him, and started to follow.

Dad had just stepped out of sight around the corner of the shed when I heard a gun shot. I couldn't tell where it came from. Dad made it to the back of the shed where he was concealed from the view of anyone that might be on the mountain to the north. I followed him around the corner and startled him, as he didn't realize I was behind him.

Dad was half crouching. He told me that he had been shot. "Where?" I asked. He said, "In my arm."

About this time Mom stepped out the door and screamed "What happened?!" Dad yelled back to her that he had been hit. Mom started screaming at the hidden snipers calling them bastards. I said "Come on Dad, we have to get to the house!" I placed my hand on his back and started pushing him in the direction of the house. He acted dazed and it seemed to take forever to get there. As I pushed him in the direction of the door, I thought to myself: *If you want to murder my Dad, you're going to have to shoot another kid in the back first!* My body was shielding him from the mountain the snipers were on. I was expecting a bullet to hit me in the back at any second. We couldn't get to the house fast enough for me.

Mom was in the doorway holding baby Elisheba and yelling for us to hurry and get inside. Kevin must have been right behind me because we all reached the door at the same time. That's when I heard, or rather felt, the second shot. It sounded as if someone had fired a gun right by my ear. I thought I had been hit as fragments of something hit my cheek. My left ear was ringing.

The sniper's bullet had passed through the glass in the door and hit my Mom in the head destroying half of her face. The bullet then hit Kevin in the left arm and lodged in his chest. Mom dropped to the floor beside me still cradling Elisheba in her arms. Kevin fell to the floor in front of me. I almost tripped over him getting in the door. Mom's still body was holding the door wide open. She had died trying to save her family.

Rachel had been standing in the kitchen and saw it all. There was blood everywhere. Thick pools spreading across the kitchen floor and into the pantry. I started screaming "Mom!" and "Kevin!" at the same time. Dad was crying, "They shot Mama! They shot Kevin and Mama!" Then, Dad, Rachel and I looked at each other and almost simultaneously cried, "The Baby!" Dad took Elisheba from Mom and handed her to Rachel. I think that was when Dad said Mom was dead.

Elisheba's face and hair were covered with her mother's blood and bone fragments. Other than that she seemed to be physically unharmed. Rachel was sobbing and saying "Mom! Mom! I can't live without Mom!"

I got down on the floor and cradled Kevin's head in my lap. I asked him where he was hurt; he said his arm and his chest, and thought he might have some broken ribs. He told me he thought he was going to die. I begged him to tell me how I could help him. He asked me to bring him water. I told him I loved him.

Dad pulled Mom's body into the kitchen and locked the door. I brought in towels from the bathroom to try and stop Kevin's bleeding. Kevin asked me for more water and a blanket.

Dad said we needed a blanket to cover Mom. I went to the living room to get one for her and for Kevin. I went back to the kitchen and walked over to Mom. I started covering her up, sobbing and saying, "I love you Mama, if you can hear me, I love you. There are no words to describe how I felt just then.

I went back to Kevin. Dad was there talking to him. He told Kevin that we weren't going to let him die if there was anything we could do about it. But Kevin told Dad that he was bleeding to death and to just let him die. He lay there on the floor like that for a couple of hours. Finally he asked Dad to help him sit up and take his jacket off. We then helped him to a chair in the living room. He continued asking for water, which we gave him.

I suddenly remembered that Dad had been wounded too. I made him take off his jacket and shirt so I could look at his arm. I could see where the bullet hit the back of his upper right arm, but I couldn't see where it came out. He said his arm was numb, but that he was okay otherwise.

We knew this was the end. They were shooting at us from unknown hiding places. They could see us, but we couldn't see them. After he put his shirt and jacket on, Dad and the three of us girls crouched on the living room floor and waited to die.

It was an awful night, decidedly worse than the last. The day before, I hadn't thought that was possible. Sam and Mom were dead, Kevin was dying, and Dad was wounded. This time we knew there would be no talking. No verbal communication. They had made that loud and clear.

54

We didn't care. They had stolen everything that was ever important to us. All they could take now was our lives.

Soon, Dad got up and moved a big recliner into the center of the living room for the little protection it would offer if they came through the front door. He closed all the curtains and blocked the front door with kitchen chairs.

We tried to quiet Elisheba with some cereal. I was sure they were going to come in at any time now and murder the rest of us. I prayed that they would just fire bomb the house and take us all at once. I couldn't watch the rest of my tattered little family die, one by one, the way it was going now. This was Hell on Earth, and we were living it.

Dad went into the kitchen where Mom's body was. I heard him crying and saying, "I love you Mama, I'm sorry, I love you." This made Rachel and I start sobbing all over again.

Kevin began to cough and continued moaning through the night. At one point he said he hurt so badly he couldn't stand it any more and asked Dad to shoot him. Dad sat in silence for minutes that seemed like hours. Rachel and I begged him not to do it. Finally Dad told Kevin he just couldn't do it. I had uncontrollable shakes for hours after that.

Later in the night we heard people moving around under the house. They were walking around in the storage room and laundry room. I was afraid they would begin to randomly shoot through the floor. Dad said he was going to yell down at them and let them know Mom and Sam were dead. He thought that maybe the snipers hadn't told any one that they had killed some of us. I didn't want him to do it because I was afraid of gunfire and didn't want him to let them know what part of the house he was in. But Dad said he had to get the word out that Mom and Sam were dead and he and Kevin were wounded.

He started yelling through the floor at them. **"You killed my wife! Vicki's dead! You murdered my boy Sam and wounded my other son Kevin! He may die tonight! You shot me in the arm! Aren't you a brave bunch of bastards?!"** There was no response. *(We know they could hear him because we later spoke to Bo Gritz through the wall using a normal tone of voice.)*

55

Elisheba would wake up crying and calling "Mama, Mama." Dad would say, "I know baby, I know, Mama's gone." I kept asking myself how this could have happened. My beautiful mother was lying dead in a pool of blood on the kitchen floor. My brother was in a shed outside, shot in the back. Kevin was sitting next to me, moaning, bleeding and expecting to die before morning. My Dad was shot in the arm. His closest friend and wife of nineteen years was gone. His son was dead.

My baby sister Elisheba would grow up never knowing her mothers love or her brother who adored her. Sam had been the first member of the family to make her smile. Rachel was even closer to Mom than I was. Her world was torn from her in an instant, an instant that took place before her eyes.

Sunday, August 23, 1992

It's morning and Kevin is still alive. Dad said it must not be his time to go. He told Kevin that he was going to try to help him. He said to Kevin, "You're going to pull out of this kid, you're going to be fine." Dad and I helped Kevin to the couch. We then cut the sleeve off of his shirt to give us better access to his wound. We tried to clean it out as best we could by pouring peroxide on it. His arm was swollen about twice it's normal size.

The actual wound in his arm was as big around as a soup can lid and raised about ¾ of an inch. We could see the bullet hole into his chest. He said he could feel broken ribs. I made him take cayenne pepper capsules to keep blood poisoning from setting in, a trick my mother had taught me. He never lost consciousness, but he was delirious at times.

Dad finally let me treat *his* wound. I doused it with peroxide and put salve on it. I placed a band-aid over the bullet hole. We didn't know there was an exit wound, Dad couldn't feel it because his arm was numb. It was two days later when Dad was looking at his jacket that he found two bullet holes. An entrance *and* an exit. After he took his shirt off again, we looked more thoroughly and discovered the exit wound in his armpit. Thankfully, there wasn't any infection.

This was the day they started using a bullhorn. They were begging us to go outside and pick up a phone that was supposed to be set up about fifty yards from the house. They would say, "Randall, Randall, come out and pick up the phone Randall. No one is going to hurt you Randall, come out unarmed and pick up the phone. You can take it back to the house and talk to us." They must have thought we were stupid. We didn't answer them when they talked to us.

Soon we heard armored personal carriers, (APC's), about twenty yards from the house. We could hear them running over things. They crushed Rachel's bicycle, the outhouse and our generator. I thought that maybe they were going to crash through the walls of our house. All during the day they continued to plead with us to pick up the phone. They even told Dad to send us kids out to get it.

We continued to care for Kevin. It was dark in the house with all of the curtains closed, so I would hold the flashlight while Dad worked on him. The smell of blood and raw flesh was making me sick. I prayed for the strength to do what was needed. Most of the time I felt as though I were in a daze. I mechanically went through the motions doing what I had to do, task, by task, minute, by minute, hour, by hour.

We used a whole bottle of peroxide on Kevin, and I gave him more cayenne capsules. I cleaned Dad's wound again as well. Once, I spotted a clump of something stuck in dried blood to Kevin's pant leg. It was some of Mom's hair. I didn't mention it to anyone. It made me cry to see it.

Rachel took care of Elisheba while I helped Dad. Elisheba slept a lot, and when she woke, Rachel would feed her canned fruit. *(I am so proud of Rach, she is such a strong, beautiful person and I love her to pieces. This is something she **never** should have had to experience.)*

Kevin kept asking for water and cigarettes. Every time Dad and Kevin lit a cigarette, I was scared that the flame would give them away and someone would shoot at them. I hated using the flashlight. Another sleepless night. I was feeling worn. I dozed for maybe an hour the entire night.

At dark they had turned floodlights on us, and left them on all night.

Monday, August 24, 1992

It's Morning. The psychological warfare starts. Today, they start trying to toy with our heads. A guy named "Fred" gets on the bullhorn and starts telling Dad to come out unarmed and pick up the phone. Then he starts telling him to send his wife or girls out. My mom was dead and they knew it. We still didn't answer them. I believed with every inch of my being (and still do) that if my dad would have stepped out the door, they would have shot him.

Kevin needed food to get his strength back. Dad crawled into the kitchen on his hands and knees. He was able to open the pantry door and bring back some canned food. There wasn't a curtain on the pantry window, and it faced the mountain the snipers were on. I was scared to death, shaking in fear, the whole time he was gone.

I said I would go to the pantry from then on. Dad tried to argue with me about it, but I insisted. I wanted to take the risk of getting shot at myself, rather than have to deal with losing another family member. So, after that, I made all of the trips to the kitchen. The worst part was having to crawl through all the blood on the kitchen floor, both Mom's and Kevin's. I made several trips to the propane stove in order to heat food and water. I hated the fact that the stove was beside the front door.

Meanwhile, "Fred" was still begging us to "communicate" as he called it. He would say, "Mrs. Weaver, Mrs. Weaver, how is the baby Mrs. Weaver? Is there anything I can do for the kids Mrs. Weaver? Why don't you just come out unarmed with the kids and end this Mrs. Weaver? Can you hear me Mrs. Weaver?" Then he would repeat the whole thing two or three times.

As it began to get dark they turned the floodlights on us. Kevin seemed slightly better. APC rigs were running all night in front of the house. I dozed off and on. We kept hearing little noises in front of the house. I wondered if at any moment gas grenades would come flying through the

58

windows to drive us out. I stayed close to my rifle. The days and nights were starting to run together.

Tuesday, August 25, 1992

It's morning and some guy with a Spanish accent got on the bullhorn. He starts saying, "Randall, Randall, Good morning Randall. How did you sleep last night Randall? I sleep pretty good I think. How are Mrs. Weaver and the children? We are having pancakes for breakfast I think. What are you having? It's a nice day Randall. Don't you think your children would like to come out and play? Get some fresh air? How about it Randall? Give yourself up." I was getting very angry at this jerk. He was worse than "Fred". They didn't need to put us through that, especially Rachel.

For the rest of the day we took care of Kevin and sat and waited. Nightfall. The generators were running. The floodlights were on.

Wednesday, August 26, 1992

Morning again. We started working on a letter telling our side of the story. We hoped someone would find it in the event we were all killed. Just in case someone cared to know the truth.

"Fred" said they were going to move a robot with a phone attached, onto our front porch. We didn't answer him, but later we heard the damn thing creeping up to the front door. It remained there until Bo Gritz removed it several days later. We couldn't see it because the curtains were closed, but we knew it was there, just waiting for one of us to make a move. Every time I went into the kitchen I could hear it hum. It sounded like an electric typewriter. I hated the thing.

"Fred" spent most of the day, trying, unsuccessfully, to get us to take the phone from the robot. Finally he said he was going to have the robot break a window and push the phone into the house. My dad started yelling at "Fred" to back off. He was afraid they would use the robot to shoot gas into the house. Dad told "Fred" to back the robot off or he would shoot the thing through the door. Fred's response was, "Okay Randall. What is it you are saying?" Dad yelled, **"Back Off!"** "Fred" said, "Okay Randall. I understand you are telling me to back off." After that, they didn't push it any further.

Now a guy named "John" took a turn on the bullhorn. He kept asking dad to communicate. Dad told me he was going to ask for his sister, Marnis. He yelled out to "John" that he would talk to his sister and no one else. "John" supposedly had a hard time hearing Dad and made him repeat the message several times.

Dad said he wanted Marnis to come up the back steps and he would let her in the back door. Now, they acted like they didn't know where the back door was. The guy would say, "Do you mean the door with the robot?" Dad kept yelling, **"No!"** Finally, "John" got it straight.

Over the bullhorn "John" says, "Randall, we are afraid that after you see your sister and get your story out you will commit suicide. You have to promise you won't commit suicide or hurt your family. Will you promise, Randall?" That made my dad angry, but he really wanted to see Marnis so he yelled, "I promise that when I see Marnis, I won't commit suicide." He had to say it several times because they "couldn't hear". Finally they said they would work on getting her from Iowa to Idaho. By then it was dark. We tried to get some rest.

Thursday, August 27, 1992

On this day, the Feds tried something new. They placed a loudspeaker under our house and played a radio message from Paul Harvey asking us to pick up the phone. They played it three times. They also played a taped message from my grandparents begging us to pick up the phone. We ignored their pleas, sensing some sort of trick. Many times "Fred" told us that there was no trick involved. "It's only a harmless telephone." He would say. "We wouldn't trick you Randall."

60

Around noon, someone got on the bullhorn and said Marnis was on her way up. They wouldn't let her near the house but put her on the bullhorn instead. The first thing Dad shouted to her was, "Marnis, Vicki's dead." They must have been relaying Dad's messages to her second hand, because they didn't allow her to hear that first one. In fact, Dad yelled out a lot of things to her that she wasn't allowed to hear. She was crying and begging us to pick up the phone. At one point she asked if everyone was okay. Dad shouted **"NO!"**. That was basically the only thing Marnis heard clearly from Dad during their limited conversation. Soon after that, she gave up trying to communicate.

Friday, August 28, 1992

By listening to the radio, we learned that the Feds had the road to our house blocked clear down at the bridge that connects the blacktop to the county road. We heard about the crowd of people gathering there in protest. Knowing that there were people there pulling for us, was a small ray of comfort in the black hole of despair we seemed to be drowning in. We also learned that among the protesters was Colonel James "Bo" Gritz. Dad shouted out that morning to whoever was listening that he would talk to Bo. It wasn't until late evening that Bo was allowed up to our house in an APC. Bo called out to dad that he was going to get out of the APC and stand near the house so it would be easier to talk. Dad yelled, "Bo? Bo, can you hear me?" When Bo said that he could, Dad yelled out to him, "Bo, my wife Vicki is dead. Kevin has been seriously wounded, and I've been shot also." Bo said something like, "Oh dear Lord" and was quiet for a few minutes. Dad then told him that it had all happened Saturday. They talked for a while longer, and then Bo said he had to go. He promised he would be back up in the morning. By that time, darkness had set in.

Saturday, August 29, 1992

Bo was back in the morning along with a friend of ours, Jackie Brown. There was also a preacher with them that we didn't know. We read to them the account I wrote of what had happened. They could hear us easily through the wall of our house. I spoke with Jackie and asked her to tell our friends and family that we loved them.

Later in the day, Dad convinced me to allow Jackie in the house. She stayed about fifteen minutes and looked at Dad and Kevin's wounds. While she was doing this, I wrote a letter to my grandparents for her to take down. She also took the copy of our story. She said she had been searched on the way up to our house, so I concealed the papers in a maxi pad so the Feds wouldn't find them and take them from her. *(I found out later that my plan had worked.)*

Bo inspected the robot on the front porch. He discovered that along with the telephone they had been begging us to pick up, it was equipped with a camera and armed with a sawed-off shotgun aimed at the phone.

Kevin said to tell Bo he would surrender only if the Feds would totally back off and leave us alone. Kevin was under the impression that he was the only one they wanted for killing Marshall Degan. I pleaded for him not to go, as I believed they would try to kill him.

That night Kevin must have been delirious. I was awake, and I heard him say, "Sara, Sara." I asked him what was wrong. He said, "Just wanted to know if you could hear me." A little while later he said, "Please don't let them take me. If they don't make the deal, don't let them take me. I don't want to go. You girls stay down. I don't want you to get hurt." I calmed him as best I could and told him he wasn't going anywhere if he didn't want to. The next morning he didn't remember saying anything.

Sunday, August 30, 1992

Bo and a good friend of his, Jack McLamb, came up and talked with us most of the morning. Dad opened the bathroom curtains and looked out at them. I was looking out too when I noticed, not thirty yards away, a guy in the weeds so well camouflaged that all I could see was his hat. It really scared me, and I begged Dad to get away from the window. He finally did.

Kevin wanted to know if the Feds were going to make that deal with him on surrendering. Jack went down to ask Glenn, the agent in charge. He came back with a written statement signed by Glenn saying that the troops would "withdraw" if Kevin surrendered. Kevin agreed to go. He stood up shakily and walked out the back door. He rested on the back porch for awhile and then Bo and Jack helped him down the steps and on to a stretcher. Then, they carried him away.

Bo and Jackie came back later with a body bag. Dad let them in the house. They put Mom's body in the bag, and Bo carried her out. He promised he wouldn't let her body touch the ground. Jackie stayed and cleaned up the kitchen floor.

Bo returned and talked with dad some more, and then he and Jackie left. We were relieved to have Mom's body out of the house. Dad took Mom's rings out of his pocket and gave them to Rachel and I. I cried most of the night.

Monday, August 31, 1992

Bo and Jack came up again and brought a letter from some friends. I didn't trust Bo and Jack completely, and pleaded with Dad not to open the door. That made Bo mad, which in turn, made me trust him even less. He kept forcefully saying that we had to surrender *that* day. Dad was considering it but I didn't want to leave. I was afraid the Feds would murder us as soon as we stepped out the door. Finally, Dad convinced me that it was best we go, and opened the door to let Bo and Jack in.

I changed my clothes, and picked up a few things. For the first time in nearly two weeks, we put our weapons down. Dad picked up Elisheba. We all linked hands and with some final urging from Bo, we stepped out into the fresh air and sunshine. I blinked and waited. I was sure there would be shots fired to kill the rest of us. We started down the steps from the back porch, and still I waited. Unbelievably, I heard nothing. We walked away from the cabin. The cabin that had been my home since I was just a child. All of my happy memories forever obscured by a huge black cloud of sorrow and pain.

I think that was the first time the reality of all that had taken place really hit me. Everything I had ever known about being a child was gone forever. The ties were broken. That was it. I could never be a kid again.

We walked down the driveway, still holding hands. That was when I saw them. The cowards in the bushes. They wore camouflage from head to toe with paint on their faces that hid everything except the smirk I saw in their eyes. I felt as though they were laughing at us. They had won. The last of our tattered little family was in their clutches. Whatever happened next was totally out of our control.

More men in camo walked up the drive to meet us. We were separated from Dad. They put him on a stretcher and strapped him down. I clutched Elisheba tightly as Rachel and I were led to a car and put in the backseat. They drove us down to the meadow. My mouth fell open in disbelief as I looked around. The meadow looked like a scene out of an army movie. There were hundreds of men in camo, a mass amount of army tents, helicopters, ATV's and ambulances. They were spread out over the meadow like a flood.

We girls were then taken to what I perceived to be the main headquarters. It was a neighbor's house. The Feds offered us juice and cookies. I guess it goes without saying that I didn't feel like eating. I walked over to the picture windows overlooking the meadow and all of it's chaos, and saw "troops" in Bermuda shorts carrying boom boxes. None of it seemed real to me. Over four hundred trained killers to take out my one little family. What a show of guts! A million dollars a day in taxpayers money, and for what? All of this to get two wounded men, and three scared girls out of their home.

A tall, middle aged, balding Fed walked up behind me. "Sara" he said. "We need to know if there are booby-traps or land mines up there." I looked him in the eye and said, "Huh, you don't **know** do you?" He then said, "Come on now Sara, we don't want anyone *else* to get hurt." I shook my head in disbelief and told him no, there wasn't anything else up there.

After that we were taken to the heart of the meadow to say good-bye to Dad as they loaded him into a helicopter; then we were turned over to our grandparents. We stood with them and waved, crying as the helicopter took our Dad away from us. The siege was over.

Words cannot describe the overwhelming feeling of gratitude I felt towards all the people who were on the other side of the roadblock as we drove through. I recognized a few familiar faces, but most of them I had never even met. Yet these people had stood firm in their belief in us, and had rallied against the injustice that had been perpetrated against us.

As we were driven to my grandparent's motel in Sandpoint, I tried to explain everything that had happened to us. At that point I'm not sure if any of it made sense to them. They lost a daughter and a grandson in an extremely brutal way. After agonizing days of waiting and worrying about the fate of the rest of us, I think they were just relieved that *our* lives had been spared.

When we got to the motel, Grandpa ordered pizza. I hadn't eaten or slept much in eleven days, and I still couldn't do either. As I watched the news on TV, I saw Dad being escorted into a jet. I wanted to go wherever it was they were taking him, I didn't want to be separated.

The plan was for my grandparents to take us back to Iowa with them and they wanted to leave that next morning. I argued, begged, and pleaded with them to let us stay in Idaho so we could be near Dad. Iowa...it seemed like a million miles away. I was only seven years old when we left there nine years earlier. I didn't remember anyone from there other than Grandma and Grandpa, because they had made a point to come visit us every year in Idaho. Everyone finally got frustrated with me and I was told to get on the plane and go to Iowa or Social Services would intervene and separate my sisters from me by putting us in foster homes. They left me with no choice. I had to relent. At the time I felt it was up to me to keep our family together. I was forced to be strong. Later, I found out that an aunt and uncle of mine had come up with the Social

Services idea to scare me into leaving Idaho. There was absolutely no truth to it. It seems like a really mean thing to do to a kid who was terrified of being separated from what was left of her family.

Letter to Mom and Sam

Dear Mom and Sam,

I miss you Mom. I can't sleep tonight because of how much I miss you. Crying doesn't seem to help. I keep getting flooded with your memories. I miss you so much. I am so frustrated because I want to remember everything about you, everything you taught me, everything you and I did together. It's not fair that you are gone. I want you back so badly.

I remember playing cards around our kitchen table at night while listening to country music. I remember how safe I felt and how loved and needed I was. You made me feel that way. You made me the person I am now and I owe you everything.

You're still gone though, and I hate it. I want to go home, but it's not home anymore because you made it home, and now you're not there. I catch myself looking for you in others, but I'm always disappointed; they never measure up.

I'm sorry Mom, sorry I didn't have the patience to let you teach me how to sew, knit and all the other things you were so good at. I remember you sewing my clothes and making my quilt. It made my bed so cozy and warm to sleep in.

How I treasure the things I did take time to learn from you, the rugs we wove, the candles we made and the food we canned.

Sam, I remember how you used to fix all of my broken jewelry. I used to tell you all of my secrets because I could trust you. We would argue and I would hate it because you were always right.

I remember the times we rode our bikes into town and I would buy you ice cream for the road home and how grateful you were because I had a job and you never had any money. We could depend on each other for anything. I feel so terrible and helpless now. I wasn't there to help you when you needed me the most. I'm so sorry.

I would give anything just to hug you both one more time and tell you I love you. That isn't going to happen though, at least not in this world.

So, I guess I'm saying good-bye.

Good-bye Mom, Good-bye Sam.
I love you.

Love,
Sara

CHAPTER

9

The Power of the Press

Get your facts first, then you can distort 'em as you please.

--Mark Twain

Today, it seems that the mainstream news media is no longer content with simply reporting the facts. They need a good story and they're not about to let truth or facts interfere with one. In some cases they're only reading a press release provided by an outside source. Too often though, the news media is a willing accomplice in the advancement of untruthful and biased information.

The following is a selection of news releases. Some of them came from the FBI and the U.S. Marshal's Service. Now that you have read the truth about what we did and didn't do, you will clearly see the government's and media's attempts to demonize us through the distortion of facts and outright lies.

MAY 6, 1992

Bonners Ferry Herald:
(Bill Dempsey, spokesman for the U.S. Marshal's Service in Arlington, Va.), "...indicated that their primary concern was to avoid such a dangerous confrontation and ensure the safety of all members of the Weaver family, especially the children."

AUGUST 22, 1992

(The day Vicki was shot and killed and the day after Sam was shot in the back)

Bonner County Daily Bee:
(Henry E. Hudson, director of the U.S. Marshals Service in Arlington, Va.) "...Degan and a group of five other marshals were on a surveillance mission when they came under fire from the remote Weaver home in the Ruby Creek area."

The Idaho Statesman:
"...The group came under fire from the fortress like Weaver home, apparently without warning."

The New York Times:
"...Only one of the deputies was hit, but the five others are still pinned down by gunfire tonight."

Spokane Spokesman-Review:
"...Two Marshals with him escaped, but two were pinned down near Degan's body by repeated sniper fire from the cabin."

AUGUST 23, 1992

Seattle Post-Intelligencer:
"...Law-enforcement officials dug in for a waiting game at the northern Idaho mountain hide-out of fugitive Randy Weaver."
"...the officers ringed the ridge in Idaho's Panhandle after an Idaho state police tactical team moved to the base of the ridge overnight and rescued three deputies who had been pinned outside the cabin since Friday."

The New York Times:
"...After the shooting, continuing gunshots from the cabin pinned down three other deputies who remained with the body till nightfall, when they were rescued by an Idaho State Police crisis response team."

AUGUST 24, 1992

The Washington Post:
"...Law officers surrounding the remote cabin of a white supremacist exchanged gunfire with people in the compound over the weekend, but the standoff began after a U.S. marshal was killed. No one was injured in the shooting Saturday."

USA Today:
"...But last Friday, authorities say, someone in the cabin shot and killed a U.S. deputy marshal during a surveillance mission."

Spokane Spokesman-Review:
"...There were reports of shots fired from the armed camp at agents and a helicopter."

AUGUST 25, 1992

USA Today:
"...Six marshals were conducting routine surveillance Friday when they unexpectedly came upon Weaver, one of his children and long-time friend Kevin Harris outside the cabin, authorities said. They said Weaver and Harris, with a dog, chased the marshals and opened fire, and a shot from Harris, 24, killed U.S. Marshal William Degan. Harris has been charged with murder. They didn't say who killed Weaver's son."

Seattle Post-Intelligencer:
"...Authorities also disclosed that Kevin Harris, the man accused of killing Marshal William Degan, was wounded Saturday by gunshots fired by federal agents from a helicopter." "Harris, 24, was shot when he emerged from the house, said Stephen Boyle, a spokesman for the U.S. Marshal's office in Washington, D.C. His condition is not known, Boyle said."

Spokane Spokesman-Review:
"...Federal agents surrounding the cabin of mountain top fugitive Randy Weaver found his 13-year-old son shot to death and lying next to the boy's rifle in a shed."

Bonner County Daily Bee:
(Gene Glenn, FBI official)   "...Glenn said he has personally been to forward perimeter where the terrain is rugged and any approach would be dangerous, especially in

light of information that Weaver is heavily armed and his house is well fortified."

AUGUST 26, 1992

Seattle Post-Intelligencer:
"...A U.S. marshal said last night 'it is a possibility' that federal fugitive Kevin Harris accidentally shot Randy Weaver's 13-year-old son during last Friday's shoot-out with deputy U.S. marshals."

"At a news conference, Idaho Marshal Mike Johnson said an autopsy on Samuel Weaver was completed yesterday afternoon, and indicated the youth died instantly from a bullet wound in the stomach."

The Idaho Statesman:
"...Also Tuesday – A Spokane, Washington, television station reported that a Boundary County autopsy revealed that the boy, Samuel Weaver died from a gunshot wound fired by Kevin Harris."

"Federal officials said Tuesday that Samuel was hit twice by bullets, possibly fired by either his father or Harris."

"A Spokane television station reported Tuesday afternoon they had confirmed reports that the 24-year-old Harris, a friend of Randy Weaver, had been shot to death."

One of the most preposterous accounts of the original shooting incident was given by John Roche, deputy director of the U.S. Marshal Service in a headline news story appearing in the *Spokane Spokesman-Review* (8-26-92).

(Roche) said, "Friday's gun battle at Randy Weaver's cabin occurred when someone drove onto the property, while federal agents watched the place." He gave this account to the *Boston Globe*:

"About noon on Friday, a car drove up to the property, and Weaver, his son, Samuel, and Kevin Harris came outside with semiautomatic rifles and their dogs to check out the visitors. At that point one of the dogs, a yellow Labrador retriever, picked up the scent of the marshals in

73

the gully about 500 yards below the cabin and began running in that direction, followed by Weaver, his son and Harris.

Marshal William Degan was hiding behind a tree stump when he saw one dog was about to attack a colleague. He jumped up, identified himself as a federal marshal and ordered the men and the teenager to halt.

The person we believe to be Harris swung around and shot, striking the deputy in the heart. When the dog tried to attack another deputy, Arthur D. Roderick, Roderick shot and killed the dog.

Roderick dove for cover in the ravine, just as a bullet believed to have been fired by Weaver grazed his coat. A third marshal, who fired three rounds, thought he hit one of the three as they were retreating. Samuel Weaver's body was found by officers in an out-building Sunday night"

Authorities on Monday would not say why they waited a day to announce the discovery. They would not speculate about why the body was in the shed but said they thought Weaver knew his son had been fatally shot.

While the gun battle with Degan and his team was going on, the second group of marshals was taking fire from others shooting automatic weapons from the cabin. One of the marshals with Degan had been trained as a medic and arrived at his side within 30 seconds. "He knew he (Degan) was dead" Roche said.

But it wasn't until 10 p.m. Friday night that a swat team, alerted by two marshals who had managed to escape from the area, could hike up the hill to evacuate Degan's body and three colleagues trapped by sporadic gunfire."

This ridiculous story was contradicted by the marshals' own testimony later in court. There is an old saying, *"You can't believe everything you hear and only half of what you see."* This could be updated to: *"You can't believe everything you read and nothing you hear from a federal official."*

Nothing can . . . be believed which is seen in a newspaper.
--Thomas Jefferson

CHAPTER

10

The Trial

If you tell the truth you don't have to remember anything.

--Mark Twain

If she (Vicki) were standing in this courtroom today, I'd go up to her and give her a big hug, and tell her I'm glad we have people who are no longer afraid of the government.

--Gerry Spence

Kevin Harris and I were tried at the same time in the federal courtroom of U.S. District Judge Edward J. Lodge in Boise, Idaho. Opening statements were made on Wednesday, April 14, 1993.

Gerry Spence, a prominent defense attorney, came to see me the first night that I was in jail. Upon shaking my hand his first comment was, "Mr. Weaver I want you to know one thing right now. I despise white supremacists." I said, "Well Gerry I'm not a white supremacist but we're on even ground anyway, because I hate lawyers." He shook my hand again and said that he also did not promise to take my case, only to look into it. If he believed I was right and the government was wrong, then he would defend me.

Several weeks into the trial Gerry looked at me and said, "Weaver, did I ever tell you why I decided to take your case? Well, you know after a couple of weeks of investigation I couldn't stand to see you lied to anymore." I said, "Right on." Then we slapped hands. I don't worship any man, but I respect a few, and Gerry Spence is certainly one of them.

During the trial, Kevin and I were held at the Ada County Jail in Boise. The U.S. Marshals Service was responsible for transporting us each day to and from the courthouse. They used a seven-vehicle convoy with a four-wheel drive Chevrolet Suburban in the front and rear of the procession. There was a SWAT team in both of these vehicles. In between, Kevin and I were in one of five Ford Crown Victorias.

The entire convoy would cruise along the interstate into downtown Boise at speeds of 60 to 80 miles per hour. At traffic lights the Suburbans would speed ahead and block traffic. Many times we would see smoke rolling off the tires of semi trucks and cars that were forced to make sudden stops to avoid hitting us.

Arriving at the courthouse, three of the cars, including the one Kevin and I were in, would race into the basement. The other vehicles would post themselves outside on guard duty. Once inside, the doors were closed and the deputies would jump out of the cars and face the cement walls in an on guard stance as if someone might jump through the walls at us. They looked ridiculous.

The paranoia on the part of the federal government throughout our ordeal was obvious in the first two months that Kevin and I were incarcerated. Each day we were moved to a different cell, sometimes twice a day. I guess the Feds thought someone might break in and try to help us escape. I believe this was done solely as a form of harassment. The jailers themselves quickly tired of this nonsense and would complain about it to Kevin and I.

For the seven months we were in jail, prior to the trial, Kevin and I were not allowed to get together or converse. The Feds, no doubt, were afraid that we would get our stories together. They, on the other hand, were most likely coached and rehearsed for those seven months and still couldn't get their stories straight. The truth is always easiest to remember and our story never changed.

No man has a good enough memory to make a successful liar.
    --Abraham Lincoln

The first witness for the prosecution was U.S. Marshal Larry Cooper. In his testimony concerning the initial shooting that killed officer Degan and my son, he contradicted the government version of events as told by prosecutor Ron Howen only the day before. He also testified that he shot Kevin Harris who "dropped like a sack of potatoes" but claims he didn't shoot Sam as he could see he was just a boy. Cooper didn't know what to say when asked, if he shot Kevin but not Sam, why was Kevin sitting in the courtroom and Sam was dead.

Cooper admitted that his weapon had a silencer on it so he could shoot our dogs without our knowledge. He had testified previously that Kevin fired the first shot killing officer Degan but couldn't explain how Degan could have then fired the seven shells found spread out over a twenty-foot area in front of Cooper's position.

Herb Byerly, the ATF agent from Spokane, passed on erroneous information that I had resisted arrest on the original gun charge and that I was involved in some bank robberies in Montana. He gave that information to the U.S.

Marshal's Service when they took over the case. Byerly described under oath how he had hired the snitch, known to me as "Gus", and instructed him to swear that that was his real name whenever he spoke to me.

When "Gus" was under oath in the courtroom, he used the name Kenneth Fadeley. Since the trial we have learned that isn't his real name either.

"Gus" testified that he would receive as much as $5000 if I were convicted. He also told how his boss (Herb Byerly) had ordered him to destroy any written instructions pertaining to the handling of my case. I'm sure those documents would have proven helpful to my defense.

U.S. Marshal Art Roderick was the team leader and third man present at the original shootout at the "Y". In his original testimony about the fatal shootout in which Sam and Marshal Degan were killed, he supported Cooper's lie by saying that Kevin Harris shot first, killing Degan, and that he had to shoot Striker because the dog was attacking him. At the time of his original testimony he did not realize that an autopsy would later be performed on the dog which proved that Striker had been shot from the rear. Therefore, unless Striker was running backwards and attacking with his hind legs, it would have been impossible for him to be shot in the rear!

Gerry Spence showed Roderick copies of sketches that Roderick and Cooper had made of the shooting scene. The drawings were supposed to have been made by each man without help from the other. With the use of transparent copies, the sketches were shown to be nearly one and the same. After lengthy cross-examination by Spence, Roderick became frustrated and barked, "The truth is the truth!" Gerry Spence said, "Yes, it is."

Dick Rogers, an FBI official in charge of their Hostage Rescue Team testified near the end of the trial. His testimony contradicted some of the earlier statements made by his own men and the U.S. Marshals. His responses to Gerry Spence's questioning during cross-examination were so snotty and hostile he was admonished by Judge Lodge to answer directly and without comment.

Rogers was one of two men who wrote the new special rules of engagement. These "rules" stated that any armed

Vicki & Sara circa 1978

Samuel age 11

Kevin & Children, Jade & Samara

Rachel, Randy, Sara and Elisheba Weaver

Presented to the Weaver family in 1996 by Idaho Citizens Awareness Network (ICAN)

Randy – Special Forces Training Group
1969

Billboard, south of Buttonwillow, CA

male around the Weaver property *"could and should"* be shot, even before a surrender announcement was to be given. When Spence asked Rogers if he knew the rules of engagement that he signed violated Idaho State law, Rogers said that he was operating under the federal codes, which preempted state law. He further claimed his actions were covered in the U.S. Codes. Spence then asked him which of the U.S. Codes allowed him to take the law into his own hands. He said he didn't know. Spence repeated the question a little louder and Rogers snapped, "The entire federal code!" I perceived Rogers to be a very cold-hearted, hostile witness. I also think it deserves mentioning that this is the same man who was in charge of the WACO tragedy which resulted in the murders of nearly 100 people, including women and children. Rogers was the first federal agent I spoke with after surrendering. He gave me a long, hard, cold stare and said in an ominous tone, "It's a damn good thing you came out now!"

At one point in the trial Spence objected when the prosecution called a witness who was a former neighbor I'd had problems with. The judge said he didn't know why he (Spence) was objecting, and added: "As far as I can see, at least 75 percent of the prosecution witnesses, so far, have helped the defense in this case."

Lon Horiuchi, the sniper who shot Kevin and I, and murdered Vicki, testified that he was required to shoot accurately enough to hit a one-quarter inch target at two hundred yards. In spite of his "required accuracy" and the use of a ten-power scope, Horiuchi testified that he was not sure if he had hit *anyone* after firing the fatal shot. He contradicted his testimony by stating that he saw *Kevin flinch* after the shot was fired. What makes this testimony so interesting (and false), is the fact that Kevin was behind the door when he was hit, and Vicki was between Kevin and the door. Horiuchi testified that he could not see Vicki standing in the doorway, but in his debriefing notes he drew a picture of the window in the door of our cabin depicting what he saw at the time he shot Vicki. His drawing clearly shows that two heads were visible through the window.

His entire testimony was given without any show of emotion or remorse. He frankly stated that he enjoyed his work. He also said that he was trying to kill Kevin Harris. Horiuchi's entrance and departure from the courthouse was under extremely heavy-armed guard.

(At the time of this writing Horiuchi has been charged with involuntary manslaughter to which he has pleaded innocent. The Justice Department has submitted a motion to have the charge dismissed and failing that, for the trial to be moved outside Idaho. The federal government contends that Horiuchi's actions were in the line of duty and he was protected by the Supremacy Clause of the U.S. Constitution.)

On June 10, 1993, the prosecution called the last of its 56 witnesses. After hearing all the lies that were told by these witnesses while under oath, it made me think of how unbelievable and actually frightening it is to think of what these guys can get away with, including perjuring themselves in court! The defense rested its case without calling any witnesses.

Our defense team filed a motion to dismiss all charges against us based on the grounds that the prosecution was attempting to convict us because of our political and religious beliefs. Ron Howen began his argument against dismissal. He stopped talking and just stood there looking down for several moments. He didn't look well. Finally he said, "I'm sorry judge, I can't continue." He left the courtroom and the judge called a short recess. His assistant, Kim Lindquist, had to continue with the argument against dismissal. We were never told exactly what had happened to Howen.

The assistant prosecutor, Kim Lindquist, insisted during his closing arguments that our political and religious beliefs had nothing to do with the prosecution of our case. He then contradicted what he had said by stating that because of our biblical beliefs we hated the government. At one point during the trial Gerry Spence told me, "This is the only trial you'll witness where the prosecution will quote bible scripture in its attempts to prosecute the defendants." Lindquist also tried to emphasize that without people willing to risk their lives by going undercover, in often-dangerous situations, many crimes would never be resolved and the laws would never be adequately enforced. My thoughts on that are that there were no crimes committed until initiated and encouraged by the snitch.

David Nevin, Kevin Harris' attorney, led off closing arguments for the defense by reciting a quote from George Washington. *"Government is not reason, it is not eloquence; it is force. Like fire, it is a dangerous servant and a fearful master."* Most of his argument dealt with the discrepancies in testimony of the many witnesses. He showed without a doubt that our story made much more sense than the government's story.

Gerry Spence began by saying, "I've been at this for over 40 years, and I've never begun a closing argument in any case with what I feel now. I just hope that I can be the best lawyer I know how to be for the next two hours and 35 minutes, because this case demands the best from all of us. You may be the most important jury that's come along for many a decade. I want you to realize that few of us, me included, ever really know how important we are or where we stand in history."

He once again summarized the defense version of what happened at Ruby Ridge the previous August. He stressed how federal agents broke very serious laws and then tried to cover them up by charging Kevin and I with crimes we did not commit. At one point when Spence was speaking of Vicki, he said, "If she were standing in this courtroom today, I'd go up to her and give her a big hug, and tell her I'm glad we have people who are no longer afraid of the government."

While speaking of the FBI sniper team, Spence said, "These are the WACO boys. This is a murder case but the people who committed the murders have not been charged and the people who committed the murders are not in this courtroom." He reminded the jurors that the U.S. Marshals Service at one time had a plan to kidnap Sara, which of course would have been illegal. Spence even referred to the ATF as the new "Gestapo in America."

By the time Spence and Nevin had finished their closing arguments I had a good feeling in my heart that the jury certainly must understand the truth in this case. However, that feeling did little to ease the nervousness I felt when the

Marshals came to us on July 8, 1993 and said, "Get dressed. The verdict is in." The jury had just completed the longest deliberation period in Idaho history lasting twenty days. The trial had received extensive coverage by several media sources.

Kevin Harris was found not guilty on all charges. He was released from custody immediately. I was found not guilty on everything except the "failure to appear" charge.

I was sentenced to 18 months in jail, a $10,000 fine, and three years of supervised probation. With my 14 months already served and 58 days off for good behavior, I was released on December 18, 1993. My fine was paid within two weeks with donations collected by Bo Gritz in Las Vegas, Nevada.

When leaving the courthouse one juror told reporters that the government's case had raised more questions than it had answered during the two-month trial. Also, since the trial I have spoken to some members of the jury who said that if they had understood the case better, they would have acquitted me on all charges. Part of their misunderstanding stemmed from the fact that Judge Lodge would remove the jury from the courtroom when the attorneys would argue over certain trial procedures and pieces of evidence that would or would not be allowed into testimony.

CHAPTER

11

Senate Hearings

The state calls its own violence law, but that of the individual, crime.

--Max Stirner

RUBY RIDGE: Report of the Subcommittee on Terrorism, Technology, and Government Information of the Senate Committee on the Judiciary

Subcommittee Members: Senator Arlen Specter, Chairman, Senator Fred Thompson, Senator Spencer Abraham, Senator Strom Thurmond, Senator Herb Kohl, Ranking Member, Senator Patrick J. Leahy, and Senator Diane Feinstein.

Participating Senators: Senator Charles E. Grassley and Senator Larry E. Craig.

(Certain parts of these excerpts that we found to be most interesting have been highlighted in bold lettering.)

INTRODUCTION

In the summer of 1995, the Senate Subcommittee on Terrorism, Technology and Government Information announced that it would hold public hearings into allegations that several branches of the Departments of Justice and the Treasury had engaged in serious criminal and professional misconduct in the investigation, apprehension and prosecution of Randall Weaver and Kevin Harris at Ruby Ridge, Idaho. The Subcommittee's inquiry into these allegations and the tragic deaths of three people in August 1992—a highly-decorated Deputy United States Marshal, Weaver's wife and Weaver's young son—was propelled by deep national concern and outrage over the events at Ruby Ridge. While the government has conducted a series of internal investigations into the charges of misconduct at Ruby Ridge, no report of any government agency has ever been released to the public.

The Subcommittee held fourteen days of hearings from September 6, to October 19, 1995, heard testimony from sixty-two witnesses, interviewed many others, and reviewed thousands of documents, including the entire transcript and exhibits from the Weaver/Harris criminal trial and various internal reports prepared by the Department of Treasury, the Department of Justice, and the Federal Bureau of Investigation. In addition, the Subcommittee posed detailed inquiries to the Attorney General, the Secretary of the Treasury, the Director of the Bureau of Alcohol, Tobacco and Firearms, the Director of the United States Marshals Service, the Director of the Federal Bureau of Investigation, the former United States Attorney for Idaho, and others concerning the role and performance of their agencies in the Ruby Ridge matter.

In fulfilling its oversight responsibilities, the Subcommittee's purposes in this inquiry were twofold. First, we sought to sift through the enormous amount of information generated about the events at Ruby Ridge in order to reach conclusions about what actually occurred and identify those responsible for any mistakes or governmental misconduct. Second, the Subcommittee sought to determine what policy changes and other reforms should be implemented or considered at the various federal agencies involved in the Weaver case.

Our efforts in this inquiry were motivated by the paramount concern that public confidence in government can be maintained only when officials at the highest levels of government are held responsible for their conduct. The Subcommittee believed that if the governments' conduct at Ruby Ridge was not subject to searching public scrutiny and analysis, and we would not have learned fully from our mistakes.

OVERVIEW OF THE EVENTS AT RUBY RIDGE

In 1986, a confidential informant for the Bureau of Alcohol, Tobacco and Firearms ("ATF") met Randy Weaver at an Aryan Nations Congress and initiated a relationship with him. Weaver ultimately sold two illegally "sawed off" shotguns to that informant in 1989. **ATF attempted to persuade Weaver to act as an informant within the white supremacist Aryan Nations, but he refused.** The United States Attorneys Office ("USAO") for the District of Idaho then indicted Weaver. Weaver was subsequently arrested and following his arraignment, released on bond pending trial. When Weaver failed to appear for trial on the weapons charge, a bench warrant and later a grand jury indictment were issued. The United States Marshals

85

Service ("USMS") then launched a seventeen-month investigation and surveillance program designed to facilitate Weaver's arrest on the weapons sale and for his failure to appear for trial.

On August 21, 1992, during a USMS surveillance mission to the Weaver property a firefight broke out between several deputy Marshals and Kevin Harris, a friend of Randy Weavers, and Randy Weaver's 14-year-old son, Sammy. When it was over, Deputy United States Marshal William Degan and 14-year-old Sammy Weaver were dead. The USMS sought emergency assistance from the Federal Bureau of Investigation ("FBI"), which immediately mobilized its elite Hostage Rescue Team ("HRT") and transported them to Ruby Ridge.

A weeklong siege of the Weaver family ensued, involving hundreds of federal, state and local law enforcement officials. On the first day of that siege, an HRT sniper fired two shots: the first hit Randy Weaver; the second killed Randy Weaver's wife, Vicki, and injured Kevin Harris. One week later, the Weavers finally surrendered. Randy Weaver and Kevin Harris ultimately were tried on numerous charges ranging from conspiracy to murder. They were acquitted on all the major counts, including the original firearm charge. Randy Weaver was convicted for his failure to appear at trial and for committing an offense (carrying firearms) while on pretrial release.

ALLEGATIONS OF GOVERNMENT WRONGDOING

Defense counsel for Randy Weaver and Kevin Harris alleged throughout the trial that agents of the ATF, USMS, and FBI were themselves guilty of serious wrongdoing during the investigation, arrest and subsequent criminal trial. Following the conclusion of the Weaver/Harris trial, the Department of Justice created a "Ruby Ridge Task Force" to investigate these allegations. On June 10, 1994, the Task Force delivered its 542-page report to the Department of Justice's Office of Professional Responsibility. That report has never been made public.[1]

---

[1] The Ruby Ridge Task Force has since released its report.

On January 6, 1995, FBI director Louis J. Freeh announced that he had either disciplined or recommended discipline for twelve FBI employees, including Larry A Potts, then Acting Deputy Director of the FBI, for their. conduct in the Ruby Ridge matter. On May 3, 1995, one of those disciplined—the FBI's on-scene commander at Ruby Ridge, Eugene F. Glenn—wrote a letter to the Justice Department's Office of Professional Responsibility, complaining that he was effectively being made the scapegoat for misconduct by higher-ranking FBI officials. As Agent Glenn asserted in his testimony before the Subcommittee, "We could say that the ship saw some hungry sharks swimming close by and they decided that they would put a few tuna out there and see if they could satisfy them.""(9/19/95 Tr. at 16-18, 57 (Glenn)).

In light of the detailed allegations by Glenn, the Department of Justice opened an Office of Professional Responsibility investigation into the events at Ruby Ridge. Since that time, a criminal referral has been made, and several high-ranking officials of the FBI have been suspended pending final resolution of that criminal investigation.

In pursuing its investigation into the events at Ruby Ridge, the Subcommittee has on every occasion attempted to avoid prejudice to the ongoing criminal investigations. In many instances we agreed to respect the request of the United States Attorney that particular subjects or documents (for example, statements by targets of the investigation) be reserved for Subcommittee inquiry at a later date. But our deference to the ongoing criminal investigation means that Subcommittee's effort to examine fully all aspects of the government's conduct in the Ruby Ridge matter is not yet finished.

(Following are Kevin's and my testimonies verbatim, as they accurately tell our side of events. The remaining excerpts are from the conclusions made by the subcommittee members at the end of the hearings.)

Randy Weaver's written testimony submitted on September 6, 1995, to the subcommittee on Terrorism, Technology and Government Information.

Chairman Specter and honored Senators, I would like to introduce you to my daughter, Sara. Two of my daughters are back home. Two of my family members are dead: my son Samuel, and my beloved wife, Vicki.

On August 21, 1992, Federal marshals shot my son Samuel in the back and killed him. He was running home to me. His last words were, "I'm coming, Dad." They shot his little arm almost off, and they killed him by shooting him in the back with a 9-millimeter submachine gun. The gun had a silencer on it. He was not wanted for any crime. He did not commit any crime. The marshals killed his dog right at his feet. He only tried to defend himself and his dog.

Sammy was just 14 years old. He did not yet weigh 80 pounds. He was not yet 5 feet tall. The marshals who killed Sammy were grown men. They were in combat gear. They had their faces painted with camouflage. They were carrying machine guns and large caliber semi-automatic pistols. They were trained to kill. Two of them were hiding behind trees and rocks in the woods where they could not be seen. The third was around a bend in the trail in thick forest. They were under direct orders from Washington to do nothing to injure the children. They were to have no contact or confrontation with my family or me. They killed him anyway in violation of their orders.

On August 22, 1992, completely without warning of any kind, a FBI sniper shot and killed my wife, Vicki. He was using a .308 caliber sniper rifle with a specially weighted barrel and a 10-power scope. He was using match grade ammunition. He had years of training to kill. I heard him testify at the trial that he wanted to kill. He shot my wife in the head and killed her. She was not wanted for any crime. There were no warrants for her arrest. At the time she was gunned down, she was helpless. She was standing in the doorway of her home. She was holding the door open for Kevin Harris, Sara, and I. She was holding Elisheba tightly

88

so she would not drop her. We took the baby from her as she lay dead and bleeding on our kitchen floor.

I am not without fault in this matter. I was convicted of failure to appear for trial on charges I had sold a sawed off shotgun to an ATF informant named Gus Magisano. He testified at trial under a different name – Kenneth Fadeley. That was probably not his real name either. I was found not guilty of the original weapons charge, and I was found not guilty of every other crime I was charged with, including murder and assault on Federal officers. I was charged with conspiring against the Government, and I was found not guilty of that charge. I was in jail for about a year before and during the trial. I have served time after the trial and now on supervised probation. I faced my accusers at a trial. I faced the FBI, the Marshals Service, the U.S. Attorney, a Federal judge and a jury of my peers. I faced the death penalty. I have been accountable for my actions. I now face you Senators to ask that those responsible for the killings of my wife and my son be brought to account for their actions.

If I had it to do over again, knowing what I know now, I would make different choices. I would come down from the mountain for the court appearance. I would not have allowed a deceitful, lying con man working for ATF to push me for almost 3 years to make a sawed off shotgun for him. I would not allow myself to be tempted in a weak moment when my family needed money. I would not let my fears and the fears of my family keep me from coming down.

But my wrongs did not cause Federal agents to commit crimes. Nothing I did caused Federal agents to violate the oath of their office. My actions did not cause Federal agents to violate direct orders from Washington. My choices did not cause Federal agents to violate their own agency policies. Federal agents have admitted to illegal acts. Judge Freeh, the head of the FBI, has made statements to the press that the so-called rules of engagement were unconstitutional. Federal agents have tried to cover-up their illegal actions.

That was their choice, not mine. I have been accountable for my choices. They should be held accountable for their wrongs. But no Federal agent has been brought to justice for the killings of Sam and Vicki Weaver.

In fact, agents of the FBI have been part of the cover-up of what really happened. One, after flunking a lie detector test, has admitted shredding documents that might clear up who authorized the death warrants on my family. I feel I have a right to know. Whether it was officials of the FBI or Department of Justice, the citizens should know who gave the shoot-on-sight orders and who approved them.

The Department of Justice has covered up what really happened by delaying, even now, the official release of two 500-page reports concerning the conduct of Federal agents at Ruby Ridge. What we know about those reports was leaked to the media, but even as we speak, Attorney General Reno and the Department Justice have still not officially released a single in-depth report about FBI and Marshal Service conduct.

The cover-up has its roots in Ruby Ridge, where Federal agents lied by telling Washington officials that the Weavers had ambushed Federal marshals and had pinned the marshals down by hiding in the trees when my boy came walking down the trail following his dog. The FBI testified of numerous grid searches of the Y using metal detectors and even using a person who was supposed to have powers as a "dowser" to find bullets with a forked stick. In all of their many searches, they found only 19 rounds fired: 3 by Kevin Harris, 2 by Sam, for a total of 5 by the boys; 1 by Marshal Roderick, 6 by Marshal Cooper, and 7 by Marshal Degan, making 14 fired by the Marshals.

Larry Cooper continued the cover-up by testifying at my trial that Kevin Harris fired the first shot. He claimed Kevin killed Marshal Degan with a 30.06. Marshal Frank Norris, who was further up in the mountain on that day, testified that the first shots were the distinctive sound of a .223, not a 30.06. Cooper testified that Mr. Degan fell over as he was shot and never got up again. That testimony was false. Evidence showed that Marshal Degan traveled over 22 feet, firing his weapon 7 times, before he was killed.

The cover-up continued during the trial. My lawyers sought records of the FBI investigation of Lon Horiuchi's shooting of my wife, myself, and Kevin Harris. They sought

90

the records long before the trial began and continued requesting them during the trial. The FBI and the U.S. Attorney did not furnish the records until after Horiuchi's testimony was completed and he had returned to Washington. Among the papers given to us late was a drawing made by Horiuchi showing that he could see people behind the door when he shot my wife. Judge Lodge was outraged and ordered that Hnoriuchi return for further cross-examination. In a rare move, he also ordered the Government to pay a fine for their conduct in delaying disclosure of that information.

Lon Horiuchi, the FBI sniper who killed my wife, said in a statement given to FBI officials on September 1, 1992, 10 days after he killed my wife, that he went through the rules of engagement in his mind just before the shooting. He decided to shoot to kill because Kevin Harris had a weapon in the vicinity of the cabin. He decided to neutralize Kevin, but the crosshairs of his sight were on the window of the door where my wife was standing. No other sniper fired. To my knowledge, Lon Horiuchi has never been disciplined in any way for killing my wife.

Some say that all of this could have been avoided if I had simply come down from the mountain and gone to trial. When I chose not to come down, I knew that I would be set up at court, just as I had been set up by the ATF. In fact, the ATF spy appeared at trial and admitted to 31 lies while he was on the stand and admitted that he was going to get a monetary settlement from ATF if I were convicted, but he would not get paid if I was acquitted. I was told at my arraignment by Stephen Ayers, a Federal magistrate, that I would probably have to forfeit a $10,000 bond if I lost my case. He said it was to pay the Government back for the cost of my court appointed attorney. That meant that if I were convicted, my family would be left destitute, penniless, and homeless. The only asset we had to pay such a debt was our home on Ruby Ridge. Judge Ayers admitted at my trial that he mistakenly quoted the law to me. There really was no law that I had to pay the Government back for my lawyer if I lost my case.

When ATF officers arrested me for selling the shotgun, they did so by pretending to be a family with car trouble.

They knew I was the kind of person who would try to help someone in trouble. It was a cold and snowy day. They were stopped on a bridge. When I walked up to try to help, several agents jumped me and threw me to the ground. A female agent, posing to be the stranded wife, threw Vicki to the ground with her face in the snow. Vicki had done nothing wrong.

Court officers confused me about the court dates. I was first told my court date would be February 19, 1991. The judge later changed that to February 20 because he did not want court staff to have to travel on a holiday. Another court official named Karl Richins, a probation officer, wrote me on February 7 and told me that my court date was on March 20. When I did not appear on February 19, an article appeared in a local paper quoting Chief Probation officer Hummel saying that no letter had been sent telling me of the March 20 court date. I provided the Senators a copy of the letter telling me the court date was on March 20.

Even though they understood my confusion and mistrust of the court system, including the mix-up over the court date, Deputy U.S. Attorney Ron Howen obtained an indictment charging me with failure to appear, and a Federal judge issued a warrant for my arrest. There was testimony at my trial that Mr. Howen obtained the indictment knowing that he would most likely have to dismiss the case because of the confusion caused by the Richins letter. Howen admitted that the Marshals Service requested that they be allowed to contact me and try to clear up the confusion before any warrant had to be served. Both the judge and Mr. Howen refused.

I wanted reassurance that I would get a fair trial, without all the deception and trickery. I wanted to know that the Government was not going to take away my home, leaving Vicki and my children homeless. I needed to know that the Government would not take our children away from Vicki if I were sent to jail. I needed to know that my wife and my children were not going to be prosecuted for any crimes. At my trial, I learned from the testimony of Marshal David Hunt that he wanted to give me assurance on all those points, but was prevented from doing so by Mr.

Howen. Mr. Howen told him in a letter dated October 17, 1991, that Marshal Hunt could not discuss these issues with me and that these issues were not proper to address unless I agreed to plead guilty to the charges.

Because of our confusion and fear and mistrust, my family made a decision that I would not come down. That decision brought the marshals to my home on the mountain on August 21, 1992. But that decision did not cause the marshals to kill my son and the FBI to kill my wife. That decision did not cause Federal agents to lie and cover-up what they had done, leading to further tragedy. That decision did not cause the FBI to send snipers to the mountain with orders to kill my family, to shoot them on sight without investigating what had happened the previous day. When the sniper killed my wife, he had not witnessed any one in my family commit a crime. No sniper or FBI agent on the mountain had witnessed any of my family commit a crime. No FBI agent had even talked with the marshals that had been involved in the shooting the previous day. The FBI sniper was executing suspects and witnesses. The FBI sniper was judge, jury, and executioner.

I am here today to do all in my power to avoid such tragedies in the future. I want the citizens of this country to learn from our tragedy so that no one else will have to suffer as my girls and I have had to suffer. I am here today to do all in my power to see that all citizens, including law enforcement officers, obey the law. I am here today because there must be accountability for the killings of my wife and son. When high-ranking FBI officials issue death warrants and cover-up their involvement, the message they send to police officers all over the country is: It is OK if you can get away with it. Citizens who cannot trust their Government band together in fear. If people in positions of power commit unlawful acts and are not held accountable, then citizens' fear of the Government is justified.

I ask you to uncover the truth about the Federal agents who have committed wrongs. I ask you to bring them to account before you. I ask you to see to it that those persons who killed my wife and my little 14-year-old son are brought to justice. I ask it for me. I ask it for my family. I ask it for my country.

Written testimony submitted on September 26, 1995, by Kevin Harris, friend of the Weaver family, to the subcommittee on Terrorism, Technology and Government Information

My name is Kevin Harris. I am 28 years old. I live in a small town in Washington State where I work as a welder. I have a 5-year old son named Jade. I completed the ninth grade in school.

I'm not a public speaker or a trained witness, and I am very nervous. My lawyers have told me that there is a great risk for me in coming here because people may misunderstand me or because I might misspeak in some damaging way.

But someone needs to tell you the truth about what happened at the Y and at Ruby Ridge, and I'm going to do that.

I didn't come here--and I never was at Ruby Ridge-- because of religion or politics. I know that a lot of people were offended by Randy's and Vicki's beliefs. But I visited the Weavers simply because they were like a family to me. They loved me and I loved them. They always welcomed me, accepted me, and made me feel that I belonged. They were warm and hospitable. There was always a place to sleep and food on the table, even when they didn't have much for themselves.

I met the Weavers when I was 16. I guess I was a troubled kid. My dad died when I was 2, and I was raised by a series of stepfathers. The Weavers permitted me to be part of their family—something which was missing from my life—and I welcomed it. I knew them, and sometimes lived with them, off and on for the next 9 years, until August 1992.

I rarely lived with them on a full-time basis. There was one period of about 8 months, beginning in the spring of 1984 right after they had finished their cabin, when I was there continuously. But mostly I came and went. I remember one period of about a year-and-a-half when I didn't see them at all.

I remember going to the cabin in late August or early September 1991. Vicki was pregnant with Elisheba, and her mom and dad came to visit. They wanted her to come down off the mountain to be near a hospital, but she refused. They made me promise to stay with the family until the baby was born in case there were problems. I stayed until the day after Elisheba was born, then left for the winter.

Sometimes I carried guns when I was at the cabin. I heard later that the marshals watched us with their spy cameras and figured out that I had a gun 66 percent of the time. The Weavers lived off the land. There was a garden, and we hunted whenever game was available. When we killed a deer, Vicki would can the venison. I also felt better having a gun in the woods, for protection from animals like mountain lions, bears, and moose, which are fairly common up there. Many people in Boundary County carry guns as a matter of course. It's not uncommon to see men, even women, carrying guns in the grocery store.

We had no idea that the deputy marshals would be in the woods on that Friday. In fact, I really didn't believe that the marshals would come up and try to arrest Randy. I figured that they would just wait him out. I mean, that's what would have made sense. When I learned at the trial that they had come to the cabin on a number of occasions, I was very surprised. Whenever I was at the cabin, I freely went to town, picked up mail, and went to the grocery store, and no law enforcement officer ever stopped me or even questioned me.

The only time I was ever contacted by law enforcement officers was the previous August, when a man who identified himself as a marshal called my foster mom in Spokane looking for me. I returned the call. The man told me, "you're probably not going to be able to help me, but I want to ask you something. What kinds of guns does Weaver have, and would he booby-trap his property?" I said, "You're right, I can't help you." He said OK and hung up.

I spent a good part of the spring and summer of 1992 at the Weaver cabin. I tried to spend a week every month or so with my son, who lived with his mother in Spokane. I came back up to the cabin the weekend before the 21st after one of these visits.

It was just bad luck that I was even at the cabin that week. I had been promised a job running equipment on a hay farm over at Ephrata, WA. The job was supposed to have begun that Monday, the 17th, but it was delayed a week. And I don't remember exactly why; the hay was wet or something or some equipment had broken down. If not for that, I wouldn't even have been there on the 21st.

Anyway, it was a typical week. I remember that I took the kids, except Elisheba, down to Ruby Creek on Thursday, and we spent the day fishing and swimming. We caught a nice mess of fish, small trout, and took them back and fried them up for dinner. Incidentally—it says here, "Incidentally, we didn't take any guns***on that trip." But I believe that I was carrying a sidearm.

August 21, 1992, was a Friday, and Friday was the day which the Weavers kept as the Sabbath. We did no work on that day—just relaxed, read, and visited.

Late in the morning we heard the dogs bark, and we went outside. Striker, the big yellow Lab, frequently barked at squirrels or noises or anything, but this was not that kind of a bark. It was more insistent, as if someone or something was around.

When we got outside to the rocks, Striker had gone on down the hill near the lower garden, and he was barking up into the woods, toward an opening where we had taken down some trees for firewood.

Sam and Randy went down the driveway, and I went down a small path through the rocks. They got to the garden area ahead of me.

By the time I got down there, Striker had come out of the woods and was at the road with Randy and Sam. He wasn't barking anymore, but he was still interested in something in the woods.

Striker started trotting down the road toward the tree line, then looking back at us as if he wanted us to follow. It's open in this area, and just before the dense trees begin, there's an old ski trail up to the right where they used to drag out logs, and Striker stopped there. Up the hill to your right after a few yards, the slope flattens out, and a game trail cuts through.

The dog headed up toward this game trail. I was thinking that an animal might be there since lots of deer come down to raid our garden. We were about out of venison, and we would have been glad to shoot a deer.

Randy and Sam and I all went to the game trail. Striker seemed to be sniffing something, and I told Randy I was going to follow the game trail. Sam said, "Me, too." Randy said he would go back and head down the other road.

Sam and I started down the game trail—the dog, Sam, and then me. The dog was walking along ahead of us, sniffing and wagging his tail, not running. He was no longer barking. He'd go ahead, then wait for us to catch up. He never got far enough ahead that we had to call him back. After a while, I figured that whatever animal had been there was probably gone.

We came out of the woods above the fern field. I immediately looked up the road thinking I might see the hind end of a deer running away. We didn't see anything, so we turned and walked down to the fern field.

The officers testified that they came out in or below the fern field, so I'm sure that Striker wasn't directly tracking them at that point.

We went through the fern field and down the road to where it connects up with the road up to the cabin, what everybody now called the Y. It's an old logging road, but it's really more of a trail. The trees grow over the top, and it's dark under them, almost like a tunnel.

The trail is fairly narrow, and we walked single file. We were just walking along, heading back to the cabin. I was carrying my 30.06 rifle in my right hand, hanging down at my side. Sam was about 10 or 15 feet ahead of me.

As we got to the Y, I saw Striker run off ahead. Suddenly I saw that he was near a person. The person had camouflage clothing on and seemed to have a beard. He wasn't looking at us. He was looking up in the direction of the road to the cabin, so I saw his profile. He had what looked like a pistol in his right hand.

At my trial I learned that the beard I saw was really a camouflage stocking over the marshal's face and that the pistol was the silenced sub-machine gun.

The dog seemed to lunge for the man's hands, the way that Striker did when you play with him. I thought about telling the man, don't worry, the dog won't hurt you, that's how he plays. But I never got the chance. I was still walking forward, and the dog was jumping around the man. The dog then moved away from the man, in a circle, and ended up racing uphill.

Suddenly the dog was shot. My impression was that the man near him was the one who shot him, but I can't be sure of that. I watched as the camouflaged man ran into the brush.

Sam stopped above the dog. As I came up next to him, he started to raise his weapon and said, "You shot my dog, you son-of-a-bitch."

As soon as he started to raise his weapon up, I turned to my right and headed for cover.

As I did, I saw smoke puffs and brass shell casings flying in the air down in the woods below the trail. I assumed Sam was shooting and that someone was shooting back at him, but I didn't actually see Sam shoot.

In fact, once I turned away from Sam as he raised his gun, I never saw him alive again. I have since learned that his shell casings were found farther up the road, so he probably wasn't shooting at that time.

I took two; maybe three steps crouched down, found some cover beside the woods. There were still shots being fired and so I fired once into the brush. I believed that whoever was in the woods was shooting at both Sam and me. I have since learned that there were at least six bullet grazes and metal fragments found in the area right behind me, so I'm sure that I was right.

I continued to move further into the woods and came up next to a stump.

Up behind me I heard Sam saying something that made me think he'd been hit. It was something like "Oh shit!" I'm not sure where he was, but I could tell he was well back behind me. I could also hear Randy yelling that we should come home, and I heard Sam say, "I'm coming, Dad." I also heard Sam say, "C'Mon Kevin, Kevin c'mon."

I heard a dull hissing sound like "thhpp" and right away I heard Sam yelp. It was the kind of sound you'd make if you were slugged in your chest with a fist. I didn't hear anything from Sam after that.

I heard moaning from the woods, and someone saying, "I'm hit, I'm hit." There was someone standing up, leaning over something, probably a person. The person standing up said, "I know, I know." Then this person jumped onto the road and said, "U.S. Marshals! U.S. Marshals!" This was the first time I'd heard anyone identify themselves. Then another man jumped up on the road and looked up in my direction. I fired my gun about 10 feet to his left. He jumped back into the brush, and I never saw him again.

Obviously, I could have shot and killed either or both of these men.

Then nothing happened for 5 or 10 minutes. I waited, frozen. I didn't hear any shooting or anything that I can recall. Then I heard a vehicle moving down below. It sounded like a rig driving up to the Y. I gathered myself and dove back further into the woods. A branch caught my hat and knocked it off. I ran deeper into the woods, and then turned uphill toward the cabin.

I ran through the woods alongside the road a ways, and then I saw Sam lying out on the road. I came out on the road above Sam. I put my rifle down on the ground and lifted up my hands, looked down toward the Y and said, "I just want to check on Sam." I walked down to where his body was, in plain view of the men at the Y.

Sam was lying face down in the road. He had on blue jeans, a white tee shirt, a flannel shirt, and a sheepskin vest, with the fuzzy side in. I rolled him over, and there was blood all over his front. His eyes were rolled back in his head, half closed. His lips were turning blue. He wasn't breathing. I felt for a pulse, and there was none. I left him lying on his back.

I learned later that Sam's right arm was shot up pretty bad, probably from when he was shot the first time, but I didn't see the arm wound then. I also learned later that the killing shot, the second shot, went right through him, from the back, and pierced his heart.

Then I picked up my rifle and headed up the hill figuring that eyes were everywhere in the woods watching me. As I got up closer to the cabin, I heard someone say, "There's

Kevin!" I tried to think of how to tell Vicki and Randy that Sam was dead, and finally I just said it. I sat down and started to cry.

They couldn't believe it. They said, "Are you sure?" I said I was sure, that I had stopped and looked at his body. Randy went kind of berserk. He grabbed his gun and fired it up into the air repeatedly. He screamed and yelled and cursed. Vicki screamed and cried. Then the girls came out, and Vicki told them what had happened.

After a while, Vicki and Randy decided that they had to go get Sam's body. I told them where he was, and I tried to talk them out of going down there. I was afraid they'd get shot, too. But they insisted on going. I stayed with the girls.

I knew when they found Sam's body because I could hear Vicki wailing and screaming, and Randy, too.

Awhile later, I heard Vicki call to me from down by the garden. She said, "Kevin, come down here, we need some help." They had gotten Sam's body to the trees, and then Randy and I got him as far as the pumphouse. Then I picked him up, put him over my shoulder, and carried him to the small cabin we called the birthing shed. I laid him on the bed where Vicki gave birth to Elisheba and left him there with his mother and father.

I understand they took his clothes off, cleaned him up, and wrapped him in a sheet, but I wasn't there for that. After a while, Vicki came out of the shed and came over to me and said, "I've never once wished that that was you and not him." Then she gave me a big hug.

For a long time after Sam was put in the birthing shed, I sat by myself on a rock ledge looking out to the east. Later I went tack to the house. The girls cried all night. I assume they didn't sleep. I know I didn't. The next morning no one talked much. We were in a daze. I remember Vicki cooking something for Elisheba, but I don't recall anyone else eating.

Early in the morning, we heard the other dogs whimpering, and Randy and Sara went out to feed them. We listened to the radio and heard that I had shot and killed a U.S. marshal.

We heard sirens in the valley. We figured they would be coming up at some point with bullhorns to demand that we come out. Late in the afternoon, we heard the dog, which was tied on the rock outcropping, whimpering like he might be wrapped up in his chain. Sara wanted to check on him, and Randy wanted to look at Sam. I needed batteries for my flashlight, and I knew there were some in a stash of Sam's personal things that he kept in a box out on the rocks, so I went with them.

Sara checked on the dog, and then followed her dad over to the shed. Suddenly there was a shot.

Weaver hollered, "I'm hit, I'm hit!" Sara started pushing him around the edge of the shed. I went straight back down the driveway. Randy was screaming, "I'm hit Ma, I'm hit!" Vicki came out of the door, halfway along the rock path, and called at us to come in. She went back to the door, opened it, then stood in it, holding it open.

Randy and Sara were ahead of me. I was running until I caught up with them, then I slowed down to their pace. I had my rifle in my left hand. As I started through the door, I heard a loud boom. I was looking at Vicki, at her face. As I heard the shot, it was as if there was something moving under her skin, then her face was deformed, almost seemed to explode.

Next thing I knew I was lying on the floor. When I couldn't feel my left hand, I realized I'd been hit.

Rachel was screaming really badly. I think she's the only one who saw what happened besides me. Randy picked the baby up, and she was all sprayed with blood and tissue. Randy handed her to Rachel, then turned to Vicki, lifted up her head, and said, "Oh, Ma***"

Vicki convulsed several times, and then was still. Randy pulled her body into the kitchen. There was a big pool of blood flowing out of her onto the floor. At first I thought it was my blood and for sure I was going to die. Sara and randy helped me take my leather coat off. My chest felt all mushy, and there was blood caked everywhere inside my coat and on my shirt.

They'd killed Sam and Vicki and almost killed Randy and me, and we were afraid that if we came outside they'd finish us all off. So we stayed inside.

101

You've heard from others about the siege. I lay in a chair for 9 days, in and out of consciousness, my wounds beginning to rot and stink. I only got up twice the whole time, both times to go to the bathroom. Both times I fainted. There were bright searchlights at night and always the voice of the negotiators, calling out to talk to Vicki, as if she were still alive.

I kept hearing on the radio that I was wanted for murder. By then Bo Gritz and Jack McLamb had come up to help out, and we were talking to them. They brought me a paper where the FBI promised that if I went out, they would leave Weaver and the girls along. I decided to go and went out with Jack McLamb.

At the hospital two FBI agents questioned me while I was on a bed, with doctors and nurses working on me. I explained as best I could while the doctors were trying to treat me what had happened at the Y. I was in the hospital for about 2 ½ weeks.

After I got out of the hospital, I was taken to Boise and placed in jail, where I was charged in Federal district court with the first-degree murder of William Degan. The prosecutors demanded the death penalty. I was amazed by what they said I was guilty of. They threw the book at me; conspiring with the Weaver family to cause an armed confrontation with the Government; assault with a deadly weapon on Roderick, Cooper, and Degan; assault with a deadly weapon on a helicopter; harboring a fugitive—Randy; aiding and abetting the possession of firearms by Randy; and using a firearm to commit these crimes.

The trial lasted about 2 months, and the Government called 56 witnesses. After that, we rested our case without calling a single witness. On July 8, 1993, after more than 10 months in custody, the jury found me not guilty of all charges.

Since that day at the Y' I have learned that Mr. Roderick and Mr. Cooper claim that we ambushed the marshals, and Mr. Cooper claims that I just wheeled and shot Mr. Degan for no more reason than that he called out to me. I want to say this as clearly as I possibly can so that there is absolutely no mistake in anyone's mind: what Mr. Roderick and Mr. Cooper say is false.

102

I would not have been anywhere near those woods if I had known that all those men with assault rifles and a silenced sub-machine gun, and who knows what other weapons, were out there. We were just walking along the trail to the Y, making a perfect target for ourselves.

If I had wanted to shoot someone, I had the perfect opportunity when I saw the man with the dog. He wasn't even looking at me. But I didn't shoot him, because I didn't have any intention of shooting anyone.

The first thing that happened at the Y is that someone shot Striker. I saw that, and I know it with complete certainty. Everything else that happened followed from that.

Marshal Thomas Norris who was on the six-man team that day reported, in his statement to the FBI and testified under oath at my trial, that the first three shots fired at the Y had the distinctive sound of a .223. And anyone who has been around guns knows that the sound of a .223 is very different from the big boom of a 30.06.

I learned later that when Marshal Hunt got down to Mrs. Rau's house he left her with the impression that the dog was shot first. Her statement to the FBI says that he told her, "Roderick finally put down the dog. Right after he put the dog down, the marshals realized they were going to be ambushed by the Weavers."

I also learned later, long after my trial had begun, that when Captain Dave Neal, of the Idaho State Police Team, got to the Y late that night and met with Mr. Roderick, that Mr. Roderick left him with the clear impression that the dog had been shot first. And after the Justice Department report came out, I learned that Mr. Henry Hudson, the Director of the U.S. Marshals Service, had the same impression.

At page 184 of the report, Mr. Danny Coulson is quoted saying that he met with Direction Hudson and two other high officials from the Marshals Service on the evening of the 21st. Mr. Hudson described the incident in this way; "One of the Deputy United States Marshals had been attacked by a dog and had shot the dog which started a firefight. During the firefight one Deputy United States Marshal had been killed."

Also, Mr. Cooper has denied all along that he shot Sam. After the FBI found Sam's body in the birthing shed, Marshal Mike Johnson said, at a press conference, that "I shot Sam in the back." They came here and told you that it was Randy but the Government's own expert witness, Dr. Fackler, said at my trial that Cooper shot Sam and he was right.

According to their story no one knew that Sam had been killed until they found his body the following week. But we, we have known all along that this was false because I and then Randy and Vicki walked down to Sam's body in plain view of the Y where the marshals were. I held up my hands and said I was going to look at Sam. Vicki and Randy cried and wailed loudly.

We learned only last week that a former Justice Department official, Mr. Jeffrey Howard, knew that Sam was dead less than 24 hours after he was killed. I understand that Mr. Hudson provided a statement to the FBI after the trial in which he said the same thing, "How could these men have known about this unless they were told by one of the marshals on the scene?"

I never met Mr. Degan but everyone says that he was a very good man and I am very, very sorry that he is dead. I do not know what his intentions were and I probably will never know. I think it is possible that he was there, that he was just like I was, in the middle of something that should not have happened, that he did not start and that was out of his control.

Sitting in that cabin for 8 or 9 days, I was not only scared of dying—in fact, at times dying did not look so bad—but I felt sure that if I did survive I would be give a meaningless trial in a kangaroo court and then sent off to prison for the rest of my life or even executed.

After all I have been through I am truly thankful for the court system that we have in this country. In many other countries in the world just the word of the deputy marshals would have been all it took to put me away forever or worse. But the court system worked. It presumed me innocent, appointed lawyers to represent me and give me a fair trial with a jury and the jury acquitted me.

I would be glad to answer any questions the subcommittee may have.

SUMMARY OF CONCLUSIONS

The ultimate responsibility for what transpired at Ruby Ridge must be shared by many people. The first, of course, is Randy Weaver himself. Had he left his mountain home and appeared in court to face the charges that were pending against him, as every American citizen should, his wife and son and a Deputy United States Marshal would still be alive today. **Weaver recognizes his mistake, and in fact candidly acknowledged it to us and to the American people on the first day of our hearings.**

But while Randy Weaver made mistakes, so did every federal law enforcement agency involved in the Ruby Ridge incident. Federal law enforcement professionals are held to a higher standard than ordinary American citizens. This country can tolerate mistakes made by people like Randy Weaver; but we cannot accept serious errors made by federal law enforcement agencies that needlessly result in human tragedy.

The Subcommittee recognizes, of course, the continuing need for strong law enforcement. We know, too, that the vast majority of federal law enforcement officers are dedicated to serving the ends of justice within the law. They put their lives on the line every day to protect the safety of all Americans, and we must never forget that. Deputy Marshal William Degan, who came upon a volatile situation that he had not created, and displayed valor and courage as he carried out his duty, is one of those people. His death is very much part of the tragedy that is Ruby Ridge.

Law enforcement cannot be strong, however, when the public loses confidence in its integrity, its judgment, and its ability to act fairly, independently, and responsibly. The public lost some of that confidence as a result of the events at Ruby Ridge. By demanding public accountability for the mistakes that were made there, and informing the American public of policy changes and other reforms that have been instituted, we hope to prevent similar tragedies in the future.

Several general themes emerged during our hearings. One is a disturbing absence of leadership from a variety of people who had responsibility for the events that led to, occurred during, and followed the August 1992 firefight and standoff. On many occasions, law enforcement officers demonstrated a disturbing lack of willingness to take charge, make difficult decisions, and then accept responsibility for the outcomes of their decisions. Too often, people in positions of authority permitted bad or uncontrolled situations to simply take their course, or inappropriately passed off decision-making authority to others.

The Subcommittee was also disappointed in the unwillingness of some high-ranking people in every agency to accept responsibility—to hold themselves accountable—for their actions and those of their subordinates. Accountability is essential to public confidence; unfortunately, many law enforcement officers who appeared before us attempted to lay the blame on others for what went wrong at Ruby Ridge. For example, we still have not satisfactorily determined the individual responsible for the Rules of Engagement that encouraged HRT snipers to shoot on sight: during our oversight hearings, no individual acknowledged ultimate responsibility for those clearly unconstitutional Rules.

There were exceptions. For example, FBI Director Louis Freeh has admitted some of the mistakes his agency made in connection with the Ruby Ridge incident and the investigations that have followed, and he has moved to institute reforms so that nothing like it can happen again. We remain concerned, however, about Freeh's questionable judgment in simultaneously reprimanding and promoting his close friend, Larry Potts, to be the FBI's Deputy Director. A good leader is not one who makes no mistakes; rather, he is someone who recognizes and admits his errors so that he can learn from them and seek to avoid their repetition.

A second theme emerges from one of our most disturbing findings: that intelligence data used by every

agency involved with the Weaver case was deeply flawed. Inaccurate or exaggerated information about Randy Weaver's conduct prior to August 1992, and his potential dangerousness was passed from one agency to another, without anyone taking the time to carefully and objectively examine what was actually known about Weaver. As Freeh described it: "...(O)ne misstatement of fact exaggerated to another one, into a huge pile of information that was just dead wrong." (10/19/95 Tr. At 73 (Freeh)). Law enforcement can never hope to make correct decisions about the apprehension and prosecution of citizens based on inaccurate or exaggerated information. Investigative agencies must find a way to do a better job in this regard—especially when they investigate people who hold unpopular religious or political beliefs. '

A third issue that crystallized during these hearings involves the basic ability of law enforcement agencies to investigate themselves fully and impartially. After reviewing numerous internal reports on the conduct of the agencies involved with the Weaver case and the Ruby Ridge incident, **we questioned whether any of the agencies can fairly and objectively investigate and criticize itself in a case of this kind.** With the exceptions of the Justice Department's Task Force Report, which was partially disavowed by the Department, and the April 5, 1995 memorandum of Deputy Attorney General Jamie Gorelick, it appeared to the Subcommittee that the authors of every report we read were looking more to justify agency conduct than to follow the facts wherever they led.

We even heard evidence that FBI agents directly violated orders on how they should draft an investigative report, in an effort to render its final recommendation unduly favorable to the FBI: Barbara Berman, who headed the Justice Department Task Force, informed us that although the FBI Inspection Division was instructed to refrain from making conclusions when it investigated the Ruby Ridge incident, the Inspection Division's Report did just that. For example, it concluded that the shots fired by Agent Lon Horiuchi were lawful. (9/22/95 TR. At 91-92, 96-97 (Berman)).

Ruby Ridge represents a tragic chapter in the history of American law enforcement. The American people expect and deserve more. If our government is to maintain—indeed, even deserve—the trust of the American people, it cannot fear or avoid the truth. The career attorneys at the Department of Justice who drafted the Department's Task Force Report, under Barbara Berman's leadership, clearly understood this. Their Report appears to be the fairest and most objective attempt to find the truth—whatever that might be, or whomever it might call to account.

BUREAU OF ALCOHOL, TOBACCO, AND FIREARMS

Many questions have been raised about ATF's conduct in connection with its pursuit of Randy Weaver for what many view as a relatively minor weapons offense. ATF's actions were the first in a string of events that resulted in Weaver's failure to appear for trial, the United States Marshals Service's efforts to arrest him, and the siege of the Weaver family at Ruby Ridge by the FBI's Hostage Rescue Team.

The Subcommittee recognizes that the ATF has in the past performed and continues to perform valuable law enforcement work. However, enough troublesome questions have been raised about its conduct at Ruby Ridge, Waco, and other places that the Subcommittee urges ATF to examine its own policies, procedures, and training more critically than it has done in the past—with a view toward fundamental reforms. The Subcommittee will hold a further hearing to consider whether ATF should remain a separate agency.

In evaluating ATF's conduct in connection with the Weaver case, the Subcommittee considered the following specific issues.

ALLEGATIONS THAT RANDY WEAVER WAS TARGETED BECAUSE OF HIS RELIGIOUS AND POLITICAL BELIEFS

Randy Weaver and others have raised the issue of whether he was "targeted for prosecution by ATF not because of any criminal conduct, but because of his religious and political beliefs--specifically his affiliation with members of the Aryan Nations, a white supremacist group. It is clear that prior to his arrest on the gun sale charges that led to the Ruby Ridge incident, Weaver had no criminal record and it is also true that the jury found Weaver not guilty of the gun sale charges on the basis of entrapment.

It is inappropriate for law enforcement agents to identify subjects for investigation or potential prosecution based on religious or political beliefs, or affiliations—no matter how odious those beliefs may be. Accordingly, we have considered carefully the claim that Weaver was inappropriately targeted.

It is clear to the Subcommittee that Weaver did not become a target for prosecution until October 11, 1989, the date on which he had a conversation with the ATF informant, Kenneth Fadeley, involving the sale of illegal shotguns—even though ATF had been well aware of Weaver's involvement with Aryan Nations for several years before that. The Secret Service had connected him with Aryan Nation's members in 1985 and he attended an Aryan Nations World Congress in 1986. (Task Force Report at 22-25). ATF denies targeting Weaver on account of his beliefs, and the Justice Department Task Force Report, which the Subcommittee has found to be the most honest and objective of the previous governmental reports on Ruby Ridge, found no evidence to support a claim of targeting. (Task Force Report at 32).

Nonetheless the question persists of whether Fadeley's pursuit of Weaver, and ATF's interest in prosecution, were motivated by the extent of Weaver's possible involvement with illegal weapons, or on account of his associations and beliefs. It is clear that ATF's standing policy is to "emphasize those violations that have the greatest potential to impact on crime and to disrupt illegal firearms activity," such as those involving armed drug traffickers and those who are "significant firearms sources to the criminal element." (ATF Order 3310.4B (Enforcement Policy)). Agent Herb Byerley, the ATF case agent, conceded to us that Weaver did not fit into the first category (9/7/95 Tr. At 12 (Byerley)), and the evidence as to the second is less than conclusive.

...Of course, at the time ATF began its investigation of Weaver, it could not know what the final outcome would be—that is inherent in the very concept of an investigation. In that context, it is important to note that the Aryan Nations and the people with whom Weaver associate—if not Weaver himself—did more than just espouse divergent political beliefs. Many had a history of actual violence, involving weapons and explosives. We believe that Weaver was targeted not so much for his beliefs, but for his association with violent people. It is clear that, after the gun sale occurred, ATF was not so much interested in prosecuting Weaver as in using its case against him as a carrot and stick to force him to become a government informant against those in political extremist groups, like the Aryan Nations, who may themselves have been engaged in significant criminal activity involving guns or explosives.

However, the distinction here—between targeting for offensive beliefs and targeting those who use their offensive beliefs to promote criminal violence—is a distinction that can easily collapse. For that very reason, special care must be taken by law enforcement agencies when investigating people like Weaver, and we are troubled here that ATF appears to have violated its own policy that incidents involving terrorist and extremist groups are to be treated as sensitive/significant investigations and therefore monitored at headquarters.)9/8/95 Tr. At 144-45 (Magaw)).

ATF Director John W. Magaw explained that Weaver was not viewed as a terrorist during Byerly's investigation. But that does not mean that the case should not have been treated as sensitive/significant. The ATF first made contact with Weaver at a meeting of the Aryan Nations—an alleged extremist group that had been involved in terrorist activities in the past. Weaver was then asked to become a government informant within that group. Had the case

110

been monitored at the headquarters level, some or possibly all of the tragedy that followed might have been avoided.

ENTRAPMENT

At his trial, Weaver was acquitted of the charge of selling two sawed-off-shotguns to ATF informant Fadeley. His only defense to these charges was entrapment, and the jury apparently believed him. ATF concedes that it was unable to convince the jury that Weaver had not been entrapped, and jurors interviewed after the trial confirmed that they believed Weaver had been entrapped. (9/8/95 Tr. At 106, 123 (Magaw)). However, the ATF denies that Weaver was entrapped, and the Justice Department Task Force found insufficient evidence, in their view, to support the claim of entrapment. (Task Force Report at 33-34).

Whether or not Weaver was entrapped, the Subcommittee is concerned that Fadeley had received virtually no training before he was sent to gather intelligence on the Aryan Nations. He was provided only the most cursory explanation of entrapment. Efforts should be made to ensure that adequate training and supervision is provided to informants who work undercover, particularly in political extremist organizations like the Aryan Nations.

COMPENSATION OF INFORMANTS

The Subcommittee considered Randy Weaver's claim that Fadeley's compensation for his work on the Weaver case depended on the outcome of the trial, and that this compensation scheme provided Fadeley with an incentive to entrap and convict Weaver. When he testified before us, Fadeley denied that he was ever told that his compensation would depend on the outcome of the Weaver trial. Director Magaw told the Subcommittee that it is not the policy of ATF to pay informants based upon convictions, and supplemented this testimony with a letter written at the conclusion of the hearings to the Subcommittee Chairman, Senator Specter.

We note, however, that on cross-examination during the Weaver/Harris criminal trial, **Fadeley testified that he did**

not believe that ATF would pay him unless Weaver was convicted. Moreover, the contracts that governed ATF's relationship with Fadeley show that the amount of money Fadeley was to receive was not determined until the trial's conclusion, when a contract was signed for his services. (9/8/95 Tr. At 138-40 (Magaw)).

ATF officials explicitly denied at the hearings and again in Director Magaw's letter that informants are paid contingent on the outcome of criminal cases. However, various ATF orders in effect through the years concerning the compensation of informants suggest that the results of judicial proceedings could be relevant to the reward given to an informant. The Subcommittee remains skeptical of Fadeley's recent recantation of his trial testimony, but it is unnecessary to make any finding based on these facts. Rather, we focus on broader policy questions raised by the possibility that Fadeley knew—or thought—he would not be paid absent a conviction.

First, we commend ATF for efforts it has initiated to revise relevant policies to make clear that no informant will ever be paid a reward contingent upon the outcome of a criminal case. (9/8/95 Tr. At 122 (Magaw)). We note with concern, however, the fact that compensation agreements are not finalized prior to the conclusion of a trial, and we are not convinced that ATF's reasons for following these procedures, outlined in Director Magaw's recent letter, are sufficient to justify them. We therefore recommend that (1) the practice of finalizing compensation agreements only at the conclusion of a trial be reviewed; and (2) all federal law enforcement agencies consider adopting a standardized policy with respect to the compensation of informants and, in doing so, determine whether the salaried approach adopted by some agencies is a more appropriate compensation method, and one that would help avoid even The appearance of impropriety.

QUALITY OF INFORMATION ABOUT WEAVERS

A theme that emerged repeatedly during these hearings related to the proliferation of false information concerning the activities of Randy Weaver and his family. This started with ATF. We examined evidence and heard testimony that ATF provided the United States Attorney's Office and the Marshals Service with inaccurate information about the danger Weaver posed to law enforcement personnel or to others.

There were three major pieces of inaccurate information that the ATF case agent passed on to the United States Attorney's office or the Marshals Service. **First, ATF agent Byerly misinformed the USAO that Weaver was "considered to be active in white supremacy activities and has been convicted of activities."** (9/7/95 Tr. At 42-45 (Byerly)). Weaver had not been convicted—or even arrested—for any crime before he came in contact with the ATF informant. Although Byerly testified that he thought the USAO was aware that Weaver was not a convicted felon, he never took any action to be sure that the USAO was informed that this information was inaccurate.

Second, there is evidence that Byerly informed the USAO that Weaver was a suspect in several bank robberies. Byerly conceded that there is a "possibility" that he did give this information to the USAO. (9/7/95 Tr. At 104-05 (Byerly)). In a memorandum from Chief Deputy Marshal Ron Evans to Chief of Enforcement Operators Tony Perez, Evans stated that the ATF case agent (Byerly) told the AUSA that Weaver was a suspect in several bank robberies. In addition, Byerly wrote in a report of investigation that "Weaver could be a suspect in several bank robberies in Spokane." **This was wholly unfounded; Weaver was not a suspect in any bank robberies.**

Third, Agent Byerly or another ATF agent informed the Marshals that Weaver had the potential to be another Bob Mathews—Mathews was an extremely violent man who had killed, bombed and robbed—and his home another Whidbey Island standoff. (9/7/95 Tr. At 79-80 (Byerly); 9/8/95 Tr. At 155 (Magaw)). Weaver had done none of these things. Of course, federal agents need to be aware of and cautious about potential threats. Nevertheless, in this case, the Mathews analogy was extreme and inaccurate.

It was this type of incorrect information and exaggeration that may have led to the decision to seek Weaver's prosecution on the gun charges in the first place.

It also may have influenced agencies, like the FBI and the Marshals Service, to overreact to the situation they were later to face—with deadly and tragic results.

Every agency involved with the Weaver case was careless at some level in the way it handled information. Without accurate information, it is impossible for law enforcement officers to make appropriate decisions with respect to the apprehension and prosecution of criminal suspects. **As we have learned from what occurred at Ruby Ridge, the results of law enforcement reliance on inaccurate information can be devastating.**

UNITED STATES MARSHALS SERVICE

INFORMATION AND INTELLIGENCE GATHERING AND TRANSMISSION

...A sixteen-page report, or "Threat Source Profile," drafted on March 7, 1991 by Senior Deputy U.S. Marshals Hunt and Mays concluded that Weaver was "extremely dangerous" and might be "deliberately seeking a confrontation with the government. . . .There maybe (sic) no turning back from a confrontational situation. Weaver appears self-destructive and willing to martyr himself for his beliefs." As the Marshals, investigation continued through the summer and early fall of 1991, this general assessment never changed significantly. Through negotiation efforts and contacts both with ATF agents familiar with the Weaver case and with friends, family, and neighbors of the Weavers, **the Marshals came to accept a portrait of Randy Weaver and his family composed variously of fact, falsehood, misinterpretation and exaggeration.** By late 1991, the Marshals believed that:

The area surrounding Weaver's home might be boobytrapped with various weapons and explosives and outfitted with tunnels or bunkers. (9/12/95 Tr. At 55 (Johnson)). This theory was based in part on what proved to be an exaggerated account of Weaver's military record and in part on uncorroborated reports from "associates" of the Weavers. (Neither bunkers nor boobytraps existed on his property.)

Weaver might be growing marijuana on his property as a source of income. Most of the information the Marshals actually received on this issue indicated that Weaver's income to the extent he had any—derived from other sources and that he was, in fact, adamantly opposed to drugs and drug use. However, based on this hypothesis, the Marshals Service was able to commission an army helicopter to conduct surveillance of the property. (9/12/95 Tr. At 94-95 (Johnson)).

Weaver was strongly affiliated with virulent antigovernment, right-wing supremacist individuals and organizations. In fact, according to a later FBI report, Weaver was affiliated with Aryan Nations only "in some limited capacity."

Weaver had made threats on the life of the President of the United States and other political leaders. (9/12/95 Tr. At 52 (Hudson)). The United States Secret Service investigated this allegation in 1985. However, in the face of Weaver's denial, they filed no charges against him, citing "lack of probable cause." (Task Force Report at 25; USMS 2/20/91 report of Investigation).

Weaver was a convicted felon and a suspect in several bank robbery cases, and was considered dangerous. Weaver also associated with a known bank robber. (9/12/95 Tr. At 51, 89-90 (Hudson)). These robberies were thought to finance white supremacist organizations, for example through the purchase of land in Idaho for use as an operations base. It was later established that these rumors were unfounded.

Weaver would not voluntarily leave Ruby Ridge to face the charges pending against him. He would kill any law enforcement official who came to arrest him. His children followed his beliefs, would defend him if any attempt were made to hurt him or take him away, and were willing to die if necessary. **This assessment was based, in part on a brief psychological profile completed by a person who had conducted no first-hand interviews and was sufficiently unfamiliar with the case that he referred to Weaver as "Mr. Randall" throughout.**

Weaver was involved with ongoing disputes with several of his neighbors, some of whom alleged that gunshots were directed toward them from the Weaver property. One of these feuds had escalated to the brink of open violence by the time of the August 21 surveillance mission, and a neighbor had threatened to take matters into his own hands if authorities did not act. (9/12/95 Tr. At 19 (Hudson)). The neighbor, Ruth Rau, reported the gunshots to local law enforcement officials, although she did not actually see where they were directed. (9/20/95 tr. At 125 (Rau)).

The Subcommittee is also concerned that, as Marshals investigating the Weaver case learned facts that contradicted information they previously had been provided, they did not adequately integrate their updated knowledge into their overall assessment of who Randy Weaver was or what threat he might pose. If the Marshals made any attempt to assess the credibility of the various people who gave them information about Weaver, they never recorded their assessments. Thus, rather than maintaining the Threat Source Profile as a living document, the Marshals added new reports to an ever-expanding file, and their overall assessment never really changed. These problems rendered it difficult for other law enforcement officials to assess the Weaver case accurately without the benefit of first-hand briefings from persons who had continuing involvement with him.

We are also concerned that it was not until the fall of 1992 and early spring of 1993 that numerous friends, relatives, and acquaintances of Randy Weaver and Kevin Harris were interviewed by the FBI, which by this time was gathering information to be used against them at trial. These range from high school teachers to old family friends to relatives, none of whom appear to have been contacted by USMS investigators during the eighteen months when Weaver was a fugitive. (9/20/95 Tr. At 104 T. Brown), 133-34 (Browns)). Had the Marshals interviewed Jackie Brown in 1991, a close family friend who regularly visited the Weavers, she would have contradicted some of the information that the Raus and others were providing concerning Randy Weaver.

Last spring, in an April 5 letter addressed to various components of the Department of Justice, Deputy Attorney

General Jamie Gorelick opined that: "The assumptions of federal and some state and local law enforcement personnel about Weaver that he was a Green Beret, that he would shoot on sight anyone who attempted to arrest him, that he had collected certain types of arms, that he had "bobby-trapped" and tunneled his property—exaggerated the threat he posed."

In fact, many of these assumptions were refuted wholesale or at least brought into question by the Marshals themselves during their investigation. But so far as we can determine, the Marshals never undertook a comprehensive reevaluation of the facts that had comprised the foundation of their initial assessment of Randy Weaver. Indeed, when the totality of the facts now known to be true about Randy Weaver is added up, his propensity for violence seems, more than anything, to have been a propensity for bluff and bluster. **The concern for his potential for violence seems to have been blown out of proportion, based on misinformation from which those having to make decisions about how to deal with Weaver assumed—incorrectly—that they were dealing with an individual with a criminal record, one with links to a number of bank robberies, rather than an individual with no criminal history whatever. We find this disturbing, and a potential contributing factor to the tragic events that occurred at Ruby Ridge on August 21 and 22, 1992.**

FORECLOSURE OF
NONCONFRONTATIONAL ALTERNATIVES

Marshals involved with the Weaver case did pursue a negotiated resolution to the standoff throughout their investigation. However, their efforts continuously were thwarted by the local United States Attorney's office ("USAO"), which refused to consider various suggestions for actions other than arrest, and which eventually shut down all negotiations. (The USAO's actions are discussed in further detail below at part C.)

Although we agree with the Justice Department Task Force's conclusion that negotiations might not have been successful in any event, we also agree that they should have been given an adequate opportunity to succeed. We commend the Marshals for their efforts to negotiate a resolution of the Weaver situation in the face of opposition from the local USAO; we only wish that they had followed their own judgment and either tried even harder to see the trial judge—who was insistent upon a quick arrest—or else pursued an appeal of the United States Attorney's decisions to the Department of Justice. The Subcommittee recognizes and regrets that the foreclosure of nonconfrontational alternatives forced the Marshals to devote resources to Weaver's case that were out of all proportion to the charges against him.

INADEQUATE PREPARATION FOR POSSIBLE CONFRONTATION DURING SURVEILLANCE MISSIONS

In a critique prepared by FBI Agent John Uda for use in a post-incident discussion between FBI Deputy Assistant Director Danny Coulson and USMS Director Henry Hudson, several concerns were raised relating to the Marshals' failure to plan for possible, though unintended, compromise of one their surveillance missions. We agree that the high number of missions carried out to develop an arrest plan may have raised the odds that a confrontation would occur. We further agree that on August 21, 1992, the Marshals approached the Weaver residence too closely, and unnecessarily made noises that risked a response without having any specific plan for retreat. (9/155/95 Tr. At 97 (Cooper)). Policies should be adopted to ensure that operations plans for future missions include adequate plans for such unanticipated outcomes.

AUGUST 21, 1992 FIREFIGHT

Who shot Sammy Weaver?
During their testimony at the hearings, Deputy Marshals Roderick and Cooper stated that they believed that Randy Weaver accidentally shot his own son (9/15/95 Tr. At 73 (Roderick); 104 (Cooper)). This contradicted what had been the government's position at the trial: that it was Marshal Cooper who had shot

118

Sammy Weaver. After hearing Marshal Cooper's testimony on this issue, the Subcommittee retained two experts to review the evidence and conduct further testing, if necessary, to determine, if possible, who shot Sammy Weaver. The Subcommittee, while it was still awaiting the results of various tests to be performed by the experts, has seen no evidence which would support the Marshals' claim but did not want to hold up the issuance of this report until those analyses are completed. The Subcommittee will release the opinions of the experts when we receive them.

In addition, since the close of the hearings, local law enforcement personnel in Boundary County, Idaho, have collected an additional forty pieces of evidence from the Y area. Analysis of this evidence may shed some light on the questions who shot Sammy Weaver.[2]

When did a Federal law enforcement officer first learn that Sammy Weaver had been shot?

The federal government has steadfastly maintained that it did not know that Sammy Weaver had been shot until his body was found in the birthing shed on August 24, 1992. The United States marshals who testified before this Subcommittee insisted that they did not know at any time on August 21 that Sammy Weaver had been shot. Randy Weaver and Kevin Harris brought that testimony into question when they said that the Marshals who were at the Y had to have seen either Sammy fall or his body lying on the ground. Randy Weaver also testified that when he and his wife Vicki walked down to the Y to bring Sammy home, they screamed and cried when they saw his body. (Because the Weavers took Sammy's body away with them, there is now no conclusive evidence of where he fell.)

In addition, Jeffrey Howard, the current Attorney General of the State of New Hampshire, testified that on the morning of August 22, 1992, when he was working as Principal Associate Deputy Attorney General at the Department of Justice, he received a call from a high ranking FBI official (perhaps Potts or Coulson) who told him that Sammy Weaver may have been shot and killed, because throughout the night, "someone on the scene had

---

[2] Later tests have proven that Cooper shot and killed Sam.

overhead the mother or Ms. Weaver wailing about her son having been shot or her son having been murdered." (9/26/95 Tr. At 118 (Howard)). In addition, Henry Hudson 302 said that Hudson learned on August 21 that Sammy had been shot. Henry Hudson denied this at the hearings and said that his 302 was wrong in this respect. (9/12/95 Tr. At 23 (Hudson)).

The Subcommittee is not able to determine conclusively when the Marshals first realized that Sammy had been shot. The marshals all denied under oath that they knew on August 21 that Sammy had been killed.

FAILURE TO TIMELY BRIEF FBI OFFICIALS

None of the Marshals who were present at Ruby Ridge on August 21 was interviewed in detail by FBI officials about what occurred that day, what they knew about Randy Weaver, or what they understood about the actual circumstances on the mountain until after the FBI's Hostage Rescue Team operation was well under way on August 22. (DUSM Dave Hunt, who was on the OP Team and therefore had no first-hand knowledge of the firefight itself, did brief local and federal law enforcement officials about what had happened. Once the Marshals were safely rescued from the mountain, they should have spoken—even if briefly—with FBI officials to inform them of whatever information might be important to the formulation of operations and arrest plans.

FAILURE TO CONDUCT COMPREHENSIVE FORMAL INTERNAL REVIEW

We were disappointed to learn that, based on his desire to avoid creating discoverable documents that might be used by the defense in the Weaver/Harris trial and his understanding that the FBI would conduct a comprehensive investigation of the incident, former USMS Director Henry Hudson decided to conduct no formal internal review of USMS activities connected with the Weaver case and the Ruby Ridge incident. (9/12/95 Tr. At 118 (Hudson)). For the same reasons, no internal shooting incident report was prepared on the August 21 firefight. In fact, the only review that has been undertaken was completed in February of this year by current USMS Director Gonzalez, who was responding to the Justice Department's task Force Report and its criticism of some aspects of USMS activities in the Weaver case.

In fact, it would have been appropriate for Director Hudson to review his agency's activities at Ruby Ridge with a critical eye in an effort to improve policies and procedures, and ultimately to prevent the kinds of mistakes that occurred at Ruby Ridge from being repeated in future cases. And while we commend Director Gonzalez for his efforts, including his work to establish formal USMS Undercover Operations Guidelines for future crises, we think his view that the Task Force Report made "no adverse findings" regarding his agency's performance is something of an overstatement. We believe this resulted in an insufficiently self-critical evaluation.

The Subcommittee is similarly disappointed that the Justice Department delayed its review of the Ruby Ridge incident until after the Weaver/Harris trial was over in late July 1993. It then took until June 1994, almost two years after the Ruby Ridge shootings, for the Ruby Ridge Task Force Report to be completed. This delay in conducting a complete review of an incident which had been the focus of intense public concern, and which resulted in the deaths of a mother and her teenage son, as well as a highly decorated Deputy Marshal, was not only unwarranted, but probably contributed to the buildup of public distrust.

UNITED STATES ATTORNEY'S OFFICE

Idaho's highest ranking federal law enforcement officer is its United States Attorney. One of the most discouraging findings we made during the hearings related to the lack of leadership exhibited by the Idaho United States Attorney's Office in connection with the arrest and prosecution of Randy Weaver.

Rather than assisting the Marshals Service in attempting to diffuse what they had concluded was a volatile situation, the United States Attorney's office placed unnecessary obstacles in the way of the Marshals' efforts to avoid a violent confrontation. For example, pretrial services incorrectly informed Weaver that his trial date was March 20, rather than February 20. Knowing this, the United States Attorney's Office nevertheless indicted Weaver on March 14 for his failure to appear—six days before the date he officially had been given. (A benchwarrant already had been issued by Judge Harold Ryan when Weaver failed to appear in February.) At least equally disturbing is the fact that prosecutors failed to inform the Grand Jury of this exculpatory evidence when they argued for Weaver's indictment.

The mistakes or poor judgment did not end there. In October 1991, the USAO ordered the Marshals to discontinue ongoing negotiations with Randy Weaver on the ground that talking to him without his attorney present violated ethical rules. Apart from the fact that this was a highly questionable conclusion, and probably at variance with existing Justice Department guidelines, the United States Attorney's Office easily could have continued the negotiations by simply bringing Weaver's lawyer into them.

Finally, the prosecutor also refused USMS Director Hudson's personal efforts in the early spring of 1992 to break what was by then a yearlong impasse. Hudson offered to speak directly with Judge Ryan to ask him to permit the Marshals to wait Weaver out rather than attempting his arrest atop the mountain. He also suggested that the USAO dismiss the indictment (at least part of which had been questionably obtained in the first place) and refile it under seal, thus also permitting the Marshals to wait Weaver out. Both of these suggestions were dismissed out of hand or ignored.

United States Attorneys and Assistant United States Attorneys should represent the highest standards of ethics and leadership in the area of law enforcement. Members of the United States Attorney's office should have taken the lead in trying to find a way to resolve the standoff without endangering either federal law enforcement agents or the Weaver family. Instead, the United States Attorney's Office pushed toward confrontation, and aggravated the situation.

FEDERAL BUREAU OF INVESTIGATION

The traditional public perception of the FBI is that it is the most professional, well-trained law enforcement agency in the United States, if not the world. **The FBI's performance at Ruby Ridge, therefore, was all the more disappointing.** It is true that all of the past mistakes made in connection with the investigation and apprehension of Randy Weaver set the stage for the FBI's actions. But the FBI then made its own mistakes and the ultimate result was the tragic killing of a mother as she held her ten-month-old daughter in her arms.

The FBI operation was marked by inadequate information gathering; the failure to take a deep breath before charging up the mountain; a focus on a tactical, rather than a negotiation response to the situation; and the use of unconstitutional shoot on sight Rules of Engagement which led to the death of Vicki Weaver. Director Louis Freeh, who was not the FBI Director at the time of the Ruby Ridge incident, has instituted certain reforms in the FBI to make sure that there is never another Ruby Ridge and the Subcommittee commends him for his actions. In certain respects, however, we have concluded that Director Freeh has not gone far enough.

INFORMATION GATHERING PROBLEMS

FBI agents who were briefed in Washington and in Idaho during the early stages of the crisis at Ruby Ridge received a great deal of inaccurate or exaggerated information concerning the Weaver case generally, and the firefight at the Y in particular. For example, Weaver was described as a former Special Forces or Green Beret member, highly trained in the use of explosives. (9/19/95 Tr. At 4 (Glenn); 9/14/95 Tr. At 26-27 (Tilton)). The FBI was told that Weaver might have built tunnels and bunkers on his property, rendering the area extremely dangerous to law enforcement officers. (9/19/95 Tr. At 5 (Glenn)).

It is true that the Marshals Service agents who had been actively involved with the case could have corrected at least some of these misconceptions. But the FBI itself is partly to blame for these problems. Even if, as the FBI claims, the Marshals who participated in the firefight did not make themselves available until mid-day on August 22, 1992, FBI officials should have demanded more timely debriefings. These lapses may have contributed to an overreaction to the crisis by those same officials.

The merit of waiting for more information is demonstrated by the fact that former Criminal Investigative Division Deputy Assistant Director Danny O. Coulson became very skeptical of the charge against Weaver and Weaver's dangerousness when, on August 23 or 24, he learned the facts from the Marshals and others at the scene. **After Coulson testified before the Subcommittee, the Subcommittee received from the Department of Justice a document that contained handwritten notes with what appeared to be the initials "DOC" after them. Special Counsel interviewed Coulson about this document. It is stamped OPR 004477 and contains a typed list of nine points followed by four handwritten notes which state:**

Something to Consider
1. **Charge against Weaver is Bull S____.**
2. **No one saw Weaver do any shooting.**
3. **Vicki has no charges against her.**
4. **Weaver's defense. He ran down the hill to see what dog was barking at. Some guys in camys (camouflage) shot his dog. Started shooting at him. Killed his son. Harris did the shooting. He is in pretty strong legal position."**

Coulson stated in the interview that the handwritten notes are his and that he may have typed the nine points himself. The document represents his reaction to the assault plan proposed by the on-site commander, Agent Eugene Glenn, a day or two after August 22, 1992. The assault plan submitted by Glenn was based on the premise that Vicki Weaver would kill her children. Coulson was not convinced of that premise and asked to know the basis for it. He was also convinced that the assault plan was otherwise faulty.

Coulson explained his handwritten notes. The basis for his comments were draft 302s and other information he received from Idaho, including interviews of the Marshals. He thought that the "charge against Weaver is Bull S___" because Weaver's crime was a minor one. When Coulson heard that Weaver had been to the Aryan nations' meeting at Hayden Lake, Idaho, he concluded that ATF was using the gun charge to try to make Weaver an informant against Butler, the Aryan Nations leader. Point two was referring to the fact that Randy Weaver had not shot at the Marshals on August 21. Similarly, point four suggested Randy Weaver's defense to the events of August 21. Randy Weaver ran down the hill to see why the dog was barking. Some men in camouflage shot his dog and killed his son. Harris—not Weaver—shot Marshal Degan. Randy Weaver, therefore, had a strong legal position. These were points that Coulson communicated to Glenn—either by faxing these notes or giving them morally to Glenn. Coulson suggested that these points be made to the Weavers in trying to talk them out of the cabin.

While the Subcommittee appreciates the need to isolate and contain suspects in the shooting death of a federal law enforcement officer, **we are unconvinced that there was any need to rush up the hill to engage in a confrontation with Randy Weaver or Kevin Harris.** The marshals who were involved with the previous day's surveillance mission had safely returned to their command post at Schweitzer Ski Resort. The Weavers had taken no hostile action for more than a day—since Sammy Weaver's death. The only danger that they posed was to law enforcement personnel who went up the mountain to confront them. These circumstances gave the FBI an opportunity to speak with the Marshals who had investigated the case and those who had been involved with the firefight, to gather other relevant intelligence, and, only then, to decide how best to proceed.

This was especially important in light of the fact that the initial purpose for deploying the Hostage Rescue Team had been to rescue the Marshals who remained on the mountain. When the Marshals were rescued, the FBI should have recognized that no one was in immediate danger—and taken a deep breath before deciding on a course of action.

INADEQUATE NEGOTIATON ALTERNATIVE

The FBI not only acted precipitously, it also stressed a tactical rather than a negotiated response to the problem. This is reflected in the operations plan that was faxed to FBI Headquarters on the afternoon of August 22, 1992. The operations plan contained no negotiation option, and it contained shoot on sight Rules of Engagement.

In the operations plan, Glenn proposed that an armored personnel carrier (APC) would first announce the FBI's intent to effect the arrest of those persons in the Weaver cabin itself. Following this destruction, the APC's would insert tear gas into the cabin; thereafter, HRT members would make an armed entry into the cabin in the hopes of arresting the adults and taking control of the children. Clearly, this initial operations plan proposed a high-risk life-threatening, direct aggressive action against the Weavers without consideration of a negotiated resolution.

It is to Coulson's credit that he rejected this operations plan "because it violated every principle of crisis management training he had undergone." (Letter from attorney for Danny Coulson to Special Counsel of Subcommittee). In Coulson's view, the first essential of any crisis situation is to isolate and contain the subject. Once this has been accomplished, law enforcement personnel should create an atmosphere for negotiations with the subjects. The prerequisite to creating such an atmosphere is to slow the process down. Glenn's plan contemplated an acceleration, rather than a deceleration, of events. It was also inconsistent with any negotiations option. Coulson, therefore, rejected the operations plan.

It was only then that former Supervisory Special Agent Fred Lanceley was asked to draft a negotiations annex for the operations plan. Lanceley, who prior to the Ruby Ridge incident had worked through hundreds of hostage crisis situations, ranging from hijackings to prison takeovers, had arrived with members of the Hostage Rescue Team in the early morning hours of August 22, 1992. **The HRT**

126

Commander, Assistant Special Agent in Charge Dick Rogers, informed Lanceley and others during a briefing that this would not be a long siege. Lanceley concluded, based_on this comment, that there would be no negotiations, and confirmed his suspicion directly with Rogers. (9/20/95 Tr. At 89-90 (Lanceley)). It was not until he was asked to draft the negotiation clause that Lanceley became directly involved with the FBI's efforts at Ruby Ridge, *Id.*, at 92. But it was already too late. The HRT sniper-observers had already been deployed up the mountain, increasing the chance that a violent confrontation, rather than a negotiated settlement, would end the standoff.

The use of an HRT robot with shotgun further demonstrates how deeply flawed the HRT operation was. On August 22, 1992, within an hour after the HRT snipers fired two shots, the FBI made a surrender announcement to Randy Weaver and delivered a telephone to the Weaver cabin using a robotized vehicle. A shotgun was attached to the robot. It should have come as no surprise to anyone that, rather than aiding the negotiation process, this equipment frightened the Weavers and slowed the negotiation process. **The Subcommittee agrees with Director Freeh that use of the robot with shotgun was the "stupidest thing I ever heard of." (10/19/95 Tr. At 95 (Freeh)). The Subcommittee notes that no one has ever taken responsibility for this.**

RULES OF ENGAGEMENT

The second major flaw of the operations plan was that it contained unconstitutional Rules of Engagement. Those Rules provided:

a. If any adult male in the compound is observed with a weapon prior to the (surrender) announcement, deadly force can and should be employed, if the shot can be taken without endangering any children.

b. If any adult in the compound is observed with a weapon after the surrender announcement is made, and is not attempting to surrender, deadly force can and should be employed to neutralize the individual.

c. If compromised by any animal (dog), that animal should be eliminated.

d. Any subjects other than Randall Weaver, Vicki Weaver, Kevin Harris presenting threats of death or grievous bodily harm, the FBI Rules of Deadly Force are in effect. Deadly Force can be utilized to prevent the death or grievous bodily injury to ones' self or that of another.

For the adult parties in the cabin, Randy Weaver and Kevin Harris, these were virtual shoot-on-sight orders. They said that agents should shoot an armed, adult male— even before a surrender announcement—if the shot could be taken without endangering the children.

These rules were inconsistent with the FBI's standard deadly force policy. As that policy was in effect in August 1992, it provided: "Agents are not to utilize deadly force against any person except as necessary in self defense or for the defense of another when they have reason to believe that they or another are in serious danger of death of grievous bodily harm. Where feasible a verbal warning should be given before deadly force is applied." At our hearings, Director Freeh and DAG Gorelick essentially conceded that Rules of Engagement were inconsistent with this. (10/18/95 Tr. At 100, 114015 (Gorelick)).

Indeed, members of a Denver FBI SWAT team deployed to Ruby Ridge during the crisis immediately recognized that Rules of Engagement were inconsistent with the FBI deadly force policy. (10/13/95 Tr. At 6 (King); 10/13/95 Tr. At 14 (Kusulas)). Special Agent Sexton understood that "if you see an adult armed male up there on Ruby Ridge, you had the green light." He said that the Rules were "out of line" and served to liberalize, rather than limit, the standard deadly force policy. (10/13/95 Tr. At 21, 28-30, 45 (Sexton)). **Other SWAT Team members, including Special Agent Donald W. Kusulas, agreed that the Rules of Engagement were not consistent with the FBI's deadly force policy. (10/13/95 Tr. At 14-15 (Kusulas)). According to Special Agent Peter K. King, the SWAT Team members felt the Rules were**

inappropriate and therefore refused to abide by them.
(10/13/95 Tr. At 15 (King)).

We also agree with the Justice Department Task Force Report that the Rules of Engagement are constitutionally informed. Again, Director Freeh and Deputy Attorney General Gorelick agree. (10/18/95 Tr. At 100, 114-115 (Gorelick)). Critical to both *Tennessee v. Garner*, 471 U.S. 1, 11-12 (1985) and *Graham v. Connor*, 490 U.S. 386, 396 (1989), the two most significant cases governing the use of deadly force, is the requirement that law enforcement officers personally and contemporaneously evaluate the risk of grievous bodily harm or death to themselves and/or others before employing deadly force. Paragraphs a and b of the Rules relieve the officer of this requirement. The language that force "should" be used encouraged the use of force without a simultaneous analysis by the officer on the scene of the threat posed by the suspect. Paragraph a also relieves the officer of the requirement of giving a warning, which *Garner* states should be done, if feasible—as it was by the time of the HRT deployment on Ruby Ridge. Paragraph d implies that the standard deadly force policy did not apply to Randy and Vicki Weaver and Kevin Harris. Rules of Engagement cannot eliminate constitutional rights with regard to certain suspects, even if they are particularly dangerous.

One of the most disputed issues is who approved the Rules of Engagement. Although he did not testify before our committee, HRT Commander Rogers previously has stated that the Rules were approved by Criminal Investigative Division Assistant Director Larry A. Potts during discussions they had while Rogers was flying across the country to Idaho. (Trial Transcript, 6/2/93 at 24-25). Potts, although he acknowledges discussing the Rules, adamantly denies having approved them as enacted.

Like Rogers, Special Agent in Charge Eugene F. Glenn also maintains that Potts approved the Rules. However, according to his testimony before this Subcommittee, it appears that while Glenn and Potts discussed the Rules of Engagement by telephone, they never discussed the precise language that would be used. It is therefore possible that

129

Glenn was talking about one set of Rules and Potts about another.

According to Potts' notes of the conversation he had with Rogers on the night of August 21, armed adults were to be considered an immediate threat under the Rules: Make every effort to avoid contact with the children. When contact made and they armed, will not fire unless it fits normal FBI firing policy of threat to life. Adults who are seen with a weapon are to be considered an immediate threat and appropriate action can be taken.

Potts testified at the hearings that, on the night he wrote these notes, he later dictated a confirmation of the Rules which stated: "This will serve to document rules of engagement agreed to by AD Larry Potts and HRT ASAC Dick Rogers at 10:25 p.m. (EDT) on 8/21/92. Every effort will be made to avoid contact with the children. If contact is made will not fire unless it becomes necessary due the threat of death or serious bodily harm. Any adult with a weapon who is observed with a weapon in the area of the Weaver home or the general location of the gun battle may be the target of deadly force." This version of the Rules never was faxed to Rogers.

We note that Potts' handwritten notes are different from the dictated, typed version. The Rules as stated in Potts' handwritten notes could be interpreted to take from officers on the scene the right to determine whether or not a particular individual posed an immediate threat. Even though Potts did not use "should" language in the second half of his handwritten notes, and instead said "appropriate action can be taken," Rogers may still have inferred from those words that it was appropriate to say that deadly force can and should be used against an armed adult.

Glenn also testified that Coulson approved the Rules when he approved the operations plan of which the Rules were a part. Coulson has admitted that he received an operations plan, which included, on page two, the controversial rule. According to Coulson, either he did not receive page two of the plan at all or he never read it, because he did not read past the first page when he rejected the plan for lack of a negotiation provision.

We think it unlikely that page one would have been faxed to Coulson without page two. If in fact Coulson received only one page of the operations plan, he certainly should have called and requested that the whole plan be re-faxed. At best, Coulson either received page two and failed to read it, or he received only page one and never called to obtain the rest of the fax. In either situation, he inadequately supervised and monitored the Ruby Ridge operation.

The Subcommittee agrees with the concern expressed by Barbara Berman, who led the DOJ-OPR Task Force investigation of the Ruby Ridge incident: **"The Rules of Engagement were in effect...from the 22nd of August until the 26th of August, and yet, inexplicably, no one at headquarters admits to having been aware of what the Rules were or having read them."** (9/22/95 Tr. at 87 (Berman)). Berman noted that the Task Force found it "inconceivable" that nobody at headquarters knew the content of the Rules of Engagement during the four days they remained in effect, because "you have people who are in the field who are acting under orders. You have operation plans that are being sent to FBI headquarters and apparently significant documents like that that are not even being read, and that concerns me." (9/22/95 Tr. At 95 (Berman)).

During their testimony, Potts and Coulson insisted that they were not in a position to approve the Rules of Engagement. According to them, the senior FBI agent on the scene—Eugene Glenn—was responsible for formulating and approving the rules. Potts and Coulson testified that their main role was in providing logistical support and coordination.

Potts and Coulson may technically be correct: in the FBI authority scheme at the time, perhaps Glenn did have the sole and sufficient authority to approve the Rules. However, from the initiation of the Ruby Ridge mission, FBI headquarters asserted a far more hands-on and substantive role in Ruby Ridge than any technical FBI authority scheme might imply. The Subcommittee is skeptical of Potts and Coulson's claim that they did not need to or could not approve the Rules, because evidently the first draft of the

131

Rules was formulated by Potts and Rogers together. Rogers himself explicitly asked Potts to draft a memorandum indicating his understanding of the Rules of Potts' approval of them. (9/21/95 Tr. At 44 (Potts)). Potts did so at FBI headquarters. When Rogers arrived at the scene, he handed Glenn the draft Rules and told him that they had been drafted and approved by FBI headquarters. Given this genesis of the Rules, it was quite natural for Glenn to look to FBI headquarters for guidance and approval for the Rules. And FBI headquarters certainly maintained a supervisory role throughout.

Although we cannot conclude on this record who (if anyone) at headquarters approved the specific language of the Rules of Engagement, Potts should nevertheless be criticized for allowing ambiguity to arise concerning an issue as critical as the Rules of Engagement. At best, his conduct was negligent. At worst, it would allow him to have the best of both worlds, taking credit for a successful operation while distancing himself from events in case of a failure. Likewise, Coulson either approved them or was negligent in not reading them. It appears that Potts and Coulson—not realizing the tragic results caused by the Rules—have distanced themselves from the approval process. **Their determination to lay the blame for what occurred on others constitutes, in our view, a deficiency in their leadership.** Potts and Coulson were ultimately in charge of the Ruby Ridge operation, and, as a result, were accountable for what occurred there. They should have accepted responsibility for whatever mistakes were made by themselves or those they supervised.

We further note that the Rules, as Potts admits approving them, suffer in part the same constitutional infirmities as present in the Rules actually used in Idaho. Potts approved a rule that adults with a weapon should be "considered an immediate threat." The Constitution requires that that determination must be made by the individual officer on the scene as he or she considers using deadly force. It should not and cannot be made from afar, or arbitrarily, as Potts did. Indeed, while the Ruby Ridge hearings were in progress, Director Freeh announced a prohibition against incorporating threat assessments into Rules of Engagement.

TWO SHOTS TAKEN BY SNIPER/OBSERVER ON AUGUST 22, 1992

The shooting of Vicki Weaver as she held her baby daughter will haunt federal law enforcement for years to come. It is this tragedy which was a central focus of the hearings. The Subcommittee explored: (1) why an FBI sniper/observer took those two shots on the evening of August 22, 1992? (2) whether he was influenced by the unconstitutional Rules of Engagement? And (3) whether either shot was appropriate under the constitution, the FBI's then current deadly force policy, or the new deadly force policy?

Horiuchi's testimony
Although Horiuchi testified for the Government at the Weaver/Harris criminal trial, he refused to do so before this Subcommittee, instead invoking his Fifth Amendment right against self-incrimination. The Subcommittee has, therefore, reviewed Horiuchi's trial testimony with great care.
At the trial, Horiuchi stated that, around 5:45 or 5:50 p.m., he heard the Weavers' dog barking, after which a young woman ran from the cabin toward the rock outcropping. The girl remained outside the cabin for approximately two or three minutes. Horiuchi did not fire because the girl was unarmed and he assumed she was a child. Soon after the girl returned to the cabin, Horiuchi observed a man on the back porch, apparently checking to see whether ponchos or blankets that were hanging there had dried. He immediately returned to the cabin. Again, Horiuchi did not shoot because the man appeared to be unarmed. Trial Transcript, 6/3/93, at 58-67.
Horiuchi testified that he heard the helicopter start its engines in the valley a few minutes after the man on the back porch returned to the cabin. The helicopter lifted off to his left and then disappeared behind some trees. Just then, three people—the young woman he had seen earlier

and two men—emerged from the house and ran in the direction of the rock outcropping. The last, whom Horiuchi identified as Harris, was carrying a long gun at high port carry. Based on information he had received at operation briefings, Horiuchi assumed these people had emerged in response to the noise of the helicopter and armored personnel carriers, to take up defensive positions along the rock outcropping. Trial Transcript, 6/3/93, at 81-87.

A few seconds later, the same man again came around the back end corner of the shed. He had his weapon at high port and was scanning the sky behind and to the right of Horiuchi's location. Horiuchi assumed he was watching the helicopter. The man moved along the shed watching the helicopter, and brought his weapon up as if trying to fire at the helicopter. The man then turned his back to Horiuchi, and seemed to be running around to the other side of the shed. Horiuchi fired his gun, and thought he hit either the edge of the shed or the man. He was not sure whether he shot the man because the man continued to move, and then disappeared behind the shed. (Trial Transcript, 6/3/93, at 88-102.

Horiuchi testified at trial that almost at the same time that Horiuchi pulled the trigger, the man made a sudden move. He grabbed the edge of the shed with his right hand, and he held up the gun in his left. Horiuchi thought that the man was trying to slow himself down to turn the corner and was using the arm with the gun to balance himself. Trial Transcript, 6/3/93, at 88-102; 6/4/93, at 36-47.

Horiuchi stated that after the first shot, he decided he would shoot at the man if given another opportunity. As the man approached the cabin door, he had his gun in his right hand, and he reached out his left arm as if to hold open the door or move someone out of the way. Horiuchi, who testified that he could not see through the window on the door, fired, and the man flinched as he disappeared behind the door. He heard a woman scream for approximately thirty seconds. Horiuchi maintains that he did not know he shot Vicki Weaver, and never intended to do so. Trial Transcript, 6/3/93, at 102-41.

Testimony of Randy and Sara Weaver and Kevin Harris

Randy Weaver told the Subcommittee that he, Sara, and Kevin Harris came out of the cabin around 5:00 p.m. on August 22, 1992 when one of the dogs barked. They walked to the rock outcropping to determine what, if anything was wrong. When the group saw nothing on the driveway, and the dog had stopped barking, Randy Weaver proceeded to the birthing shed to visit his son's body. (9/6/95 Tr. At 110-12 (R. Weaver)). Harris went to retrieve a battery Sammy kept in a box near the rock outcropping.

Randy Weaver walked around the shed and did not see anything. He shifted his rifle to his left hand and was reaching up to turn the latch to open the shed door when he was shot in the back. Because the shot sounded so loud, Weaver thought the shooter was directly behind him. He turned around, but did not see anything: all was quiet. Weaver maintains that, had they heard a helicopter at this moment they all would have run back to the cabin immediately. (9/6/95 Tr. At 11-12 (r. Weaver)).

When Randy Weaver was shot, Sara came running around the corner of the shed, and they began to run back toward the cabin, Sara pushing her father ahead of her. Vicki appeared, to find out what had happened. She shouted for everyone to return. She was holding her baby daughter, Elisheba, in her arms. Vicki then returned to the porch, opened the door, and held it open for everyone. Harris came from the rocks and fell in behind Randy and Sara. Just as Harris stepped in the door, however, Randy heard a shot. Sara was pushed into the cabin, and Kevin fell in behind her. Vicki was lying on the step leading from the cabin to the porch. Harris' testimony at the hearing was consistent with Randy Weaver's. (9/6/95 Tr. At 110-12 (R. Weaver)).

The bullet Horiuchi fired had entered through a pane of glass on the cabin door. Weaver stated that the curtains were open, but hanging loosely at the time of the shot. Sara also claimed that the curtains were open and that she believed Vicki Weaver could have been seen from the other side of the door. (9/6/95 Tr. At 196-99 (Sara Weaver)).

Testimony regarding the helicopter

Law enforcement officers at Ruby Ridge had reports that the Weavers or Kevin Harris previously had threatened aircraft operating in the area. For example, after the firefight on August 21, but before they returned down the mountain late that night, the Deputy Marshals reported that they heard gunfire as a plane flew overhead.

HRT Commander Richard Rogers, who did not appear before this Subcommittee, instead invoking his Fifth Amendment right against self-incrimination, did testify in the Weaver/Harris case. In describing the path of the helicopter, he stated that "(t)he helicopter came up, again trying to stay out of the shooting area of this— potential shooting area of this cabin." Trial Transcript, 6/2/93, at 63-64. He further testified that the helicopter was "exposed and had a fairly good view" of the cabin for ten or fifteen seconds. *Id.*

Helicopter pilot Frank Costanza informed this Subcommittee that he always flew at least two hundred yards away from the perimeter of the compound in an effort to stay out of the line of fire although he sometimes remained within the danger zone. He stated that he flew in a manner that exposed the helicopter in different places for no longer than six-to-twelve seconds. (9/19/95 Tr. At 110-15 (Costanza)). Thus, he spent a total of no more than a minute exposed to potential fire from the Weavers.

Horiuchi's testimony at the Weaver/Harris trial reveals some confusion in his own mind as to whether the helicopter actually was threatened when he took his first shot. He admitted that he was aware at that time that nobody had fired on the helicopter during earlier missions the same day. Trial Transcript, 6/4/93, at 4-5. In addition, although Horiuchi assumed that Weaver was looking in the direction of the helicopter when he fire, he did not know the exact position of the helicopter throughout the incident. Trial Transcript, 6/3/93, at 69-70; 6/4/93, at 130. It is also unclear whether Horiuchi believed that the helicopter was within rifle range—and therefore in danger—given his lack of knowledge about the helicopter's actual position. Finally, on cross-examination, Horiuchi was questioned about a flight he had taken before ascending the ridge. **Horiuchi testified that "(I)t wasn't necessarily out of rifle range, a good shot could have hit the helicopter anytime we showed up;" But in previous testimony, Horiuchi also had said that "(w)e stayed well** out of range of the cabin during the flight." Trial Transcript, 6/4/93, at 73-75.

Testimony regarding position of curtain

The shot went through the window and the curtain on the cabin door. The set of curtains was hung on the inside of the door, one on the cabin door. The set of curtains was hung on the inside of the door, one on each side of the window. The bullet passed through a pane and one of the curtains on the right side of the window, looking at the door from the outside.

At trial, Horiuchi testified that he did not know whether the curtains were open or closed. In an attempt to resolve the issue, the government called Bruce Wayne Hall, an FBI forensic scientist specializing in soil, glass, and building materials. Hall testified that the "bullet was fired at approximately a right angle to the glass. The curtain was in line with the path of the bullet, the bullet passed through the glass, passed through the curtain, and consequently deposited glass in line." He acknowledged that he could not and did not know the position of the other curtain at the time of the shooting. Trial Transcript, 6/4/93, at 46, 49-50.

On cross-examination, Hall acknowledged that when the curtain was in the position in which he believed it was at the time of the shooting, that he could still see the jury on the other side of the door, *Id.* At 70. He also admitted that he did not know whether the curtain with the hole was pinned back at the time of the shot; apparently, the hole can line up with the hole in the window even with the curtain pinned back. *Id.* At 73. He conceded that he did not know whether the curtains ere wide open or shut at the time of the shot. *Id.* at 77.

Horiuchi testified that he could see Weaver's face looking up at the helicopter through his telescopic sight at the time of the first shot. Whether he could see similar detail at the cabin door would seem to depend on the position of the door, whether the curtain was open, the angle at which he was looking, and the power of his telescopic sight. Law enforcement officials speaking on this subject, however, appear to agree that due to weather conditions and the late hour of day, Horiuchi could not, in fact, see what was happening behind the door. Sara Weaver, however, disagrees. (9/6/95 Tr. At 199, 202 (S. Weaver)).

Legality of the first shot

Under the Supreme Court's reasoning in *Tennessee v. Garner,*490 U.S. 386 (1989), Horiuchi's first shot would be constitutional if objectively reasonable. Thus, if Weaver or Harris posed "no immediate threat to the officer and no threat to others, the harm resulting from failing to apprehend (them) does not justify the use of deadly force to do so." *Garner,* 471 U.S. at 11. All FBI reports and the Justice Department Task Force Report concluded that the first shot was objectively reasonable, and therefore, constitutional. Similarly, every FBI and Justice Department witness at the hearings has supported the legality of the first shot. Although we are not prepared to conclude that the first shot was unconstitutional, we are concerned for several reasons that the perception of an imminent threat to the helicopter was not what caused Horiuchi to take the first shot, and that Horiuchi was influenced in taking the first shot by the Rules of Engagement.

First, as reflected in his direct testimony, Horiuchi's understanding of the Rules of Engagement and his justifications for firing the shots raise a real question as to whether he had properly evaluated the threats faced by the law enforcement officials. On direct examination, Horiuchi testified as follows:

Question. Could you have shot him?

Answer. Yes, sir, I could have.

Question. Did you shoot at him?

Answer. No sir, I did not.

Question. Why did you not?

Answer. Sir, again, I was searching this area here with the naked eye, again because of the field of view of the

138

scope was very limited. He surprised me when he came around the corner, because at that time I saw three people come out and three people disappear, so I assume all three of them would stay together. When I saw one individual come around the corner I was not on my rifle scope, and by the time I got to my rifle scope, he was already moving around the corner out of my sight.

Question. Had you been on your rifle scope when you saw what you had, would you have taken a shot?

Answer. Probably not, sir.

Question. Well, at that time it would have been a quick shot because by the time I got to my rifle scope he was already moving, and there was no really threatening movement at that time.

(Trial Transcript, 6/3/93, at 86-87).

In his cross-examination, Horiuchi further testified:

Question. You said that you assumed that he was trying to get around the birthing shed to perhaps take a shot?

Answer. Yes, sir.

Question. You thought maybe he was getting ready to take a shot, didn't you?

Answer. At what time, sir?

Question. At the time you shot him?

Answer. At the time, I shot him, sir? No, sir.

Question. You didn't think he was getting ready to take a shot then?

Answer. During that period he was attempting to take a shot, or I assumed he was attempting to take a shot.

Question. Assume he was attempting to take a shot?

Answer. Yes, sir.

Question. He was not getting ready to take a shot at the time that you took your shot?

Answer. No, sir.

Question. You also testified it was your assumption that he intended to shoot the helicopter?

Answer. Yes, sir.

Question. You were wrong about all of those things?

Answer. Would you repeat that question?

Question. He wasn't a threat to you or the helicopter?

Answer. Yes, he was a threat, sir.

Question. You were waiting to kill the people that came out of the house, weren't you?

Answer. If they came out of the house and provided a threat, yes, sir, we were.

Question. You were waiting to kill them irrespective of a threat, weren't you?

Answer. Based on the Rules of Engagement, sir, we could.

Question. Based on the Rules of Engagement the decision had already been made that he was a threat?

Answer. Yes, sir, a Marshal had been shot, sir.
Trial Transcript, 6/4/93, at 78-80).

As is common in adversarial proceedings, parts of Horiuchi's trial testimony can be read to support the view that he fired in response to a perceived threat, while other parts suggest that the Rules of Engagement led him to fire on Randy Weaver and, later, Kevin Harris (when he killed Vicki Weaver) without particular regard to the current presence of any threat. The Subcommittee respects agent Horiuchi's decision to invoke his constitutional privilege not to testify before us. That means, however, that conclusions about his motivation will have to be drawn from a cold record, rather than the live testimony of a witness whose credibility could be individually assessed by each Subcommittee member.

That said, the Subcommittee is nonetheless left with the impression that Horiuchi's shots, especially the second, might well not have been taken if the FBI's standard deadly force policy, rather than the special Rules of Engagement, was in effect. Significant portions of Horiuchi's testimony—that he did not shoot an individual he saw poking at the ground with a stick because "by the time I got to my rifle scope he was already moving," (Trial Transcript, 6/3/93, at 86); that he did not shoot when he reached his scope "because there was no really threatening movement at what time," (Trial Transcript, 6/3/93, at 86-87); and that he did not shoot the three individuals when they first emerged from the cabin "because it was a complete surprise that they came out," (Trial Transcript, 6/3/93, at 78); that "the decision that we were already in

140

danger *had already been made for us* prior to going up the hill[,]" (Trial Transcript, 6/3/93, at 165 (emphasis added)); and, most particularly, that "[b]ased on the Rules of Engagement we could...[kill them irrespective of a threat] (Trial Transcript, 6/4/93, at 30);"—raise concerns for us that, at a minimum, the interplay between the special Rules of Engagement and the longstanding FBI deadly force policy, created ambiguity where there should have been none and may have led to a shot where there was no real present danger.

That Horiuchi may well have fired because of the Rules of Engagement and not because of any particular threat posed by the individuals is also suggested by a section of Horiuchi's grand jury testimony, read by defense counsel at the trial, in which Horiuchi stated that the snipers had agreed that: "[I]f only one subject came out, we were going to pretty much wait...a minute, 30 seconds, maybe more before anyone took the shot to try and eliminate having taken one shot and then the rest of them pretty much all inside. We wanted them all outside if we were going to shoot the two subjects." Trial transcript, 6/4/93, at 17. Similarly, in an FBI interview on December 30, 1993, sniper Jerome Barker "recalled generally some kind of discussion on waiting until more than one subject was out of the building before any shots were taken, but [could not] recall the timing or context of the discussion." (Barker 12/30/93 FBI Form 302).

Our concern over the possibility that the Rules of Engagement superseded standard deadly force policy is heightened by contemporaneous statements from other HRT members. In an August 31, 1992 statement, Horiuchi's partner, Dale Monroe stated that "we had a 'green light' " to use deadly force against an armed adult male. (Monroe 8/31/92 FBI Form 302). Similarly, sniper Edward Wenger stated that his "understanding of the [Rules of Engagement] was that if I saw an armed adult outside the residence, I was to use deadly force against that individual." (Wenger 10/28/92 FBI Form 302). Sniper Christopher Whitcomb stated that the "Rules of Engagement were that if, before the occupants of the cabin

141

were notified that they were to surrender, the male adult occupants were seen carrying weapons, deadly force could be used." (Whitcomb 8/31/92 FBI Form 302). Finally, sniper Mark Tilton stated that "[w[e were told...we should use deadly force if no children were endangered." (Tilton 8/31/92 FBI Form 302). Indeed, as Horiuchi's partner Dale Monroe described his own conduct on Ruby Ridge only ten days after the incident: "During the entire incident, I was trying to focus on the armed, adult males in order to fire at them but could not get a clear shot because of the vegetation near me and the movement of the subjects." (Monroe 8/31/92 FBI Form 302).

Second, we are not fully convinced that the helicopter was actually in any danger or that Horiuchi necessarily believed that it was. Horiuchi testified at the Weaver trial that he did not know exactly where the helicopter was flying. In fact, the helicopter pilot, Frank Costanza, has stated that it is extremely difficult for ground observers to ascertain the location of an airborne helicopter from its engine sounds, particular in settings like Ruby Ridge, "due to echoes and resonance created by surrounding hills, rocky terrain, and, in this case, low cloud cover." (Costanza 9/10/92 FBI Form 302). Indeed, the prosecutor had this exchange with Horiuchi on direct examination:

Question. When you saw the activity in the house area, could you tell from the sound where the helicopter was at that particular time?
Answer. Generally, sir, it was either behind me or to my right or to my left.
Question. You couldn't see the helicopter at the time you saw the activity, is that correct?
Answer. No, sir, once the activity started, I was concentrating on the three individuals that came out of the building, not the helicopter.
Trial Transcript, 6/3/93, at 69-70.

Furthermore, it is not clear that the helicopter was in range of a rifle shot. The HRT helicopter flew six missions near the Weaver cabin on August 22 and never received fire. On cross-examination, Horiuchi was questioned about the flight that he took prior to ascending the ridge. Horiuchi first claimed that [I]t wasn't necessarily out of rifle range, a good shot could have hit the helicopter anytime we showed up." (Trial Transcript at 7898). Testimony from the helicopter pilot, Frank Costanza, during the hearing did confirm that he had at some point come within rifle shot range of the cabin (9/19/95 Tr. at 110-15 (Costanza)). Here, again, however, the record is ambiguous. During trial, defense counsel then asked Horiuchi to read from a previously made statement. In that statement, Horiuchi said that "[w]e stayed well out of range of the cabin during the flight." *Id.*

Thus, there is a reasonable basis to conclude that the Rules of Engagement, more than any fear for the safety of the helicopter, prompted Horiuchi to take the first shot. We agree with the Justice Department Task Force Report that the Rules of Engagement created an offensive atmosphere—one in which the snipers/observers were more likely to employ deadly force than had the standard deadly force policy been in effect. Deputy Attorney General Gorelick testified at the hearings that the Rules of Engagement "had to have affected the point of view that [Horiuchi] brought to the incident." (10/18/95 Tr. at 124 (Gorelick)). It seems altogether plausible that the combination of offensively-oriented Rules of Engagement and exaggerated reports of Randy Weaver's dangerousness would lead a sniper/observer to more readily use deadly force than when operating under the normal deadly force policy and with no heightened sense of dangerousness.

It has been suggested that the helicopter was knowingly used to lure the Weavers out of their home so that hey could be shot under what on its face was a shoot to kill policy. Glenn acknowledged this perception when he testified before us. (9/19/95 Tr. at 15 (Glenn).

The Subcommittee concludes, however, tat there is no credible evidence on which to base a judgement of such serious culpability on the part of federal law enforcement persons. All credible evidence suggests that the helicopter was used for legitimate purposes. It had been sent up several times during the day to enable the FBI to understand the terrain that the agents would face as they went up the mountain.

Legality of the second shot.

The Subcommittee believes that the second shot was inconsistent with the FBI's standard deadly force policy and was unconstitutional. It was even inconsistent with the special Rules of Engagement.[3]

We do not believe that there is any credible evidence that the three individuals who were running into the cabin presented a threat of grievous bodily harm or death to Agent Horiuchi or anyone else. The three were running for the cover of the cabin. They had not returned the sniper's fire and, according to Horiuchi's trial testimony, they were running faster than when they emerged from the cabin. (Trial Transcript, 6/3/93, at 105). The FBI had not previously considered the Weavers and Harris a significant threat from within the cabin. The FBI had decided to accept the risks posed by these suspects as they remained in their cabin, in making plans to negotiate with them while they remained inside. The helicopter had taken several flights earlier in the day, and the Weavers had not shot at it from the cabin. The second shot, therefore was not objectively reasonable. Under *Garner* and *Graham*, the use of deadly force was not necessary, and therefore, was not constitutional. The Subcommittee found persuasive the testimony of Justice Department Task Force leader Barbara Berman on this point. (9/22/95 Tr. at 110-11 (Berman)).

Moreover, the Subcommittee questions whether the second shot was justifiable even under the operative Rules of Engagement, which permitted deadly force, only "if the shot can be taken without endangering any

---

[3] Senator Feinstein dissents from the conclusions that Special Agent Horiuchi's second shot was unconstitutional and outside the Rules of Engagement. The Rules of Engagement clearly said that deadly force can and should be used on armed adult males, which was exactly what Horiuchi was doing when he fired the second shot at Kevin Harris. Agent Horiuchi had to make a split-second decision, in dangerous circumstances. Hindsight is often better, but there was no evidence presented to suggest that Horiuchi violated either the deadly force policy or the Rules of Engagement.

children." Horiuchi's second shot, which went through the cabin door and killed Vicki Weaver, missed the 10-month-old baby in her arms, Elisheba, by less than two feet. Even accepting as true Horiuchi's trial testimony that he could not see into the cabin when he fired that shot, Horiuchi should have known that as he fired "blind" through the cabin door, he was shooting into an area which could well have contained Vicki Weaver and her two younger daughters. We fail to see any reasonable basis for a judgment that a high powered rifle shot through an opaque door into an area that could hold a mother and several children, including an infant, could have been undertaken without endangering the children. In addition, he should have realized that Sara had just run into the house and that there was a possible bottleneck at the doorway.

The Weavers claim, however, that Horiuchi was not shooting "blind;" that he must have known that Vicki Weaver was behind the door because she had come outside after the first shot and because she was visible through the open curtains on the door. Horiuchi denied at trial that he could see beyond the door itself. (Trial transcript, 6/3/93, at 105). The Subcommittee recognizes that conditions including the overcast weather, the late time of day and the overhang above the porch which might have created a shadow over the door, may well have made it unlikely that Horiuchi could see what was behind the door.

Moreover, curtains attached to the door window may have also obstructed Horiuchi's view. The testimony at the Weaver/Harris trial with respect to the curtains was not dispositive. The government's expert could not say with certainty whether the curtains were or were not tied back at the time of the shooting. In addition, while testifying at the Weaver trial, the expert admitted that he could see the jury even when the curtains were not tied back because there was a space between the two panels of the curtains. Sara Weaver testified at the hearings that the curtains were tied back. We also note that the curtain ties were observed on the floor of the porch in photographs taken by the FBI after the Weavers surrendered but were not included with the evidence taken from the cabin.

The Subcommittee, however, does not believe that Horiuchi saw Vicki Weaver (or her baby) behind the door or that he knew that they were there. Although the Subcommittee did not hear directly from Horiuchi and therefore had no opportunity to judge his credibility for ourselves, on the basis of his trial testimony and the physical evidence, we do not believe that Horiuchi intentionally killed Vicki Weaver.

The Subcommittee questioned FBI Director Freeh at length about the propriety of the second shot. **In the early part of his testimony, Freeh seemed reluctant to denounce the second shot (10/19/95 Tr. at 27-34 (Freeh)). However, in his later testimony Freeh acknowledged that the second shot should not have been taken, as he put it, "for policy and for constitutional reasons."** (10/19/95 Tr. at 183 (Freeh)).

The Subcommittee concludes without reservation that the second shot should not have been taken. We believe that under the circumstances on August 22, as Randy and Sara Weaver and Kevin Harris ran back to their cabin, there was not the kind of immediate or imminent threat of real harm to others that could have justified deadly force. The snipers were concealed and remote. Even if a helicopter was present, it could not have been at risk from individuals fleeing headlong into a cabin after they had been shot at. There was simply no justification then present for the use of deadly force, while there was considerable risk of danger to the Weaver children.

The Subcommittee urges the FBI, indeed all federal law enforcement agencies, to review their own policies, training and procedures to prevent the use of deadly force in circumstances similar to the Ruby Ridge second shot. Law enforcement officials authorized to use deadly force must be taught to make a critical calculation of the immediacy or imminence of the threatened harm at the time the force is to be used—or in the circumstances that might have been present at some point earlier, or that might hypothetically occur later. Officers must be trained to include the risk to innocent third parties, especially children, as a critical factor in their own decisions over whether to fire their weapons.

146

The Subcommittee believes an important distinction must be noted. We have no wish to second-guess the many thousands of fine local, state and federal law enforcement officers who put their lives on the line every day to protect our communities. We do not want in any way to hamstring the police officer involved in a hot pursuit or close range confrontation with a dangerous criminal. Those women and men have to make snap judgments every day, and we have no wish to increase their personal risk by requiring undue hesitation before they protect themselves.

But in the case of the snipers on Ruby Ridge, no such personal or immediate danger existed. When Horiuchi fired, he was in a concealed, safe and remote firing position. He had time to think before he shot, time to be briefed before he was deployed, and time to calmly plan his actions. Under those circumstances, what Horiuchi saw as Weaver, Harris and Sara fled back toward their cabin—where one child (two, as far as law enforcement officers were aware) and one infant were present—gave him insufficient justification to fire his weapon.

It is not our purpose to urge (or to urge against) prosecution or other sanction against Agent Horiuchi. But it is the Subcommittee's firm purpose to make sure that in the future, in similar circumstances, inappropriate and unconstitutional deadly force like the second Ruby Ridge shot will never again be used.

INACCURACY OF FBI 302 FORMS

FBI agents prepare 302s to record the contents of investigatory interviews after the completion of each interview. They are prepared in all FBI investigations, not just internal ones. **The Subcommittee is deeply troubled by testimony we heard that some 302s prepared in relation to the Weaver case and the Ruby Ridge incident did not accurately reflect what witnesses told the FBI agents who interviewed them.** Among the disputed 302s were those of Deputy Marshal Cooper, former Marshals Service Director Hudson, and former Marshal Michael Johnson.

147

Former Director Hudson's 302 noted that Hudson learned late on August 21 that Sammy Weaver was thought to have been injured during the firefight that day. Marshals Service personnel and FBI agents all now say that they had no idea Sammy had been hurt until they discovered his body in an outbuilding on the Weaver property days later. When asked about his discrepancy during the hearings, Hudson informed us that his 302 was inaccurate on this point. (9/12/95 Tr. at 23 (Hudson)).

Former U.S. Marshal Johnson's 302 did not reflect, according to Johnson, the full scope of his interview. Specifically, Johnson informed FBI agents interviewing him that Former Deputy Attorney General George Terwilliger may have had some involvement with approving the controversial Rules of Engagement that governed FBI HRT activities at Ruby Ridge through August 26, 1992. (9/12/95 Tr. at 41-45 (Johnson)). His 302 nowhere reflects this discussion, however.

Most disturbing, perhaps, is the controversy that developed over Deputy United States Marshal Cooper's 302, which was revised because Cooper believed it did not accurately reflect what he told FBI agents. In its first, iteration, the 302 noted that Kevin Harris was carrying a weapon with a blue steel barrel during the firefight (he was not; Sammy Weaver was); and that, after the firing was over, Cooper saw Kevin Harris walking up the trail toward the Weavers' residence. In a later version which Cooper actually dictated, Cooper stated that he saw Kevin falling after he shot his rifle in Kevin's direction, but that he saw Sammy running up the trail after he fired his last bullets. This discrepancy was raised during the Weaver/Harris trial and was used by the defense to discredit Cooper's testimony. (Trial Transcript, 5/26/93, at 211-228 (Venkus); task Force Report at 473-75).

The testimony of three different witnesses that information in their 302s was inaccurate or missing is sufficient to convince the Subcommittee that, while alterations to witness statements as reflected in 302s related to the Ruby Ridge incident may not have been intentional, some inaccuracies did occur. The Subcommittee believes that the FBI should begin to record witness interviews at least in internal investigations. Tapes of witness interviews will permit FBI agents to more accurately reflect witness statements in 302s and will permit adequate review of the accuracy of the information recorded on 302 forms.

CRIME SCENE INVESTIGATION

Much was made by the attorneys who represented Randy Weaver and Kevin Harris at their criminal trial concerning the way evidence was collected around the Y area after the shooting incident. Special Agent Joseph Venkus (now retired) coordinated the search there.

At trial, the Weaver-Harris lawyers emphasized the facts that the Y area was not secured after the shooting incident and that many vehicles were permitted to drive through it before any search was conducted. Special Agent Venkus made no effort to determine how many vehicles or people had been through the area before the search began. In fact, the first agent who arrived for the search, Special Agent Mark Thundercloud, commented that the dog Striker, who had been killed during the firefight, had been run over by a government vehicle.

Moreover, accepted methods of marking where evidence is located were not employed during the searches. Thus, Special Agent Thundercloud was not able to determine the distance between the northernmost and southernmost bullets that were fired by Marshal Degan before he died. At least one important piece of evidence—a bullet—was removed and then replaced by FBI agents coordinating the search.

During the hearings, Supervisory Special Agent James J. Cadigan acknowledged that the crime scene investigation "was not as organized" as he was accustomed to (10/13/95 tr. at 77-78 (Cadigan)). The Marshals argued that their version of the facts about the shootings at the Y could be supported if an adequate search of the area between the Weaver cabin and the Y were conducted, although according to Special Agent Venkus, they personally assisted with searches of the area. (10/13/95 Tr. at 163 (Venkus)).

The Subcommittee agrees that a more careful search and evidence-gathering process would have left us with far fewer questions today.

ALLEGATIONS OF COVER-UP

In July 1995, the Justice Department, during its continuing inquiry into government misconduct in connection with the Ruby Ridge incident, uncovered information that E. Michael Kahoe, a former subordinate of Larry Potts, had destroyed documents relating to the conduct of Potts and other high-ranking FBI officials during the August 1992 standoff with Randy Weaver. Louis Freeh soon suspended Kahoe. But unanswered questions about this alleged cover-up, including who might be involved and how far it extends, remain.

On August 11, 1995, four additional FBI officials involved with the Ruby Ridge incident also were suspended, including Larry Potts and Danny Coulson. This occurred one day after a criminal referral to the United States Attorney's Office in the District of Columbia. Due to a reported conflict of interest within that USAO, Michael R. Stiles, the United States Attorney for the Eastern District of Pennsylvania, took over the investigation in Washington. Since then, one additional agent has been suspended. It is unclear what was learned in the intervening month between the Kahoe suspensions and those of Potts, Coulson and the others, that caused the additional administrative action.

When the Subcommittee initiated its investigation into the Ruby Ridge incident, the Justice Department expressed concerns that our actions could interfere with possible future prosecutions related to the alleged cover-up. Although we were unwilling to delay this public airing for an indefinite period until all possible administrative and judicial action had been taken against various people involved with the Ruby Ridge incident and its aftermath, we appreciated the Justice Department's concerns, and therefore carefully avoided any inquiry that might compromise its efforts: we took great pains to avoid using compelled statements of people who may be subject to prosecution, thus permitting their use in future prosecutions under *Garrity* v. *New Jersey*, 385 US. 493 (1967); we met several times to confer about the proceedings; and we accepted most of the Department's decisions to ' withhold documentary evidence that conceivably might impact the investigation. However, a full public airing of this matter must eventually be undertaken, and when the investigation is concluded the Subcommittee will consider additional hearings to deal with the cover-up allegations and related issues.

THE FBI LABORATORY

The Subcommittee examined closely various criticisms of the FBI Laboratory reported by sources including the United States Attorney's office for the District of Idaho, components of the FBI, the United States Marshals Service, local law enforcement agencies, and the trial court in *United States* v. *Weaver*. The Subcommittee was particularly concerned by the Department of Justice Task Force conclusion that a "lack of coordination, communication, and coordination" within the FBI and with the United States Attorney's Office had a significant adverse impact on the government's preparation for trial and on the way that the government was perceived by the court and by extension, the public, in the Weaver criminal trial. (Task Force Report at 296,300).

Cooperation with other governmental actors

The Subcommittee is also concerned by the testimony of a representative of the FBI Laboratory that, in the Weaver case, the Laboratory received requests for examinations that fit what they saw as the prosecutors' "theory of the week" and that the resulting tension between the prosecutors and the case agents adversely affected the coordination necessary between the field and the laboratory for effective and timely processing of evidence. (10/13/95 Tr. at 68-69 (Cardigan)).

Oversight of the FBI laboratory

The Subcommittee has questions about the effectiveness of oversight of the FBI Laboratory by the FBI's own Inspection Division. In August 1992, at about the same time as the Ruby Ridge incident, the Inspection Division inspected the FBI Laboratory and reported that it was operating "efficiently and effectively." Yet, soon after the FBI gave its own Lab a clean bill of health, criticisms started rolling in. First the prosecutors in the Weaver/Harris case complained about the Lab. Then, in June 1994, the Justice Department's Task Force criticized the Lab, and the Justice Department's Inspector General raised serious questions about the Lab in an audit report. It seems that a more thorough inspection would have noted some of these same problems.

THE FBI's FAILURE TO COMPLY WITH
DISCOVERY OBLIGATIONS

The Subcommittee concurs in the view that the FBI failed to comply with its discovery obligations in the Weaver/Harris case. This was not a case of innocent mistake or even excusable negligence; rather, the FBI willfully and repeatedly failed to abide by discovery rules and irreparably damaged the government's presentation of evidence at the criminal trial. Where, as here, the FBI assumes "the role of an adversary" to the USAO, rather than a partner in the prosecution of criminal charges (Task Force Report at 407), something has gone terribly wrong.

Failure to produce relevant documents
During the course of the Subcommittee hearings, it became clear that the FBI had never provided several crucial documents to either the USAO or defense counsel for Randy Weaver and Kevin Harris. For example, the FBI never produced its After Action Report, the handwritten or typed versions of Assistant Director Potts' notes regarding the Rules of Engagement, or the handwritten notes of Deputy Assistant Director Coulson concerning the strength of the allegations against Randy Weaver. Indeed, it is possible that had Weaver and Harris been convicted at trial, the nondisclosure of some of these materials could have resulted in a reversal on appeal.

In light of the USAO's position that in the interest of justice it would permit modified "open file" discovery in the Weaver/Harris case (9/15/95 Tr. at 160 (Ellisworth)), denial of these materials to the defendants was not a matter for the FBI to determine unilaterally. Such disclosure may well have been mandated by decisions of the United States Supreme Court (e.g. *Brady* v. *Maryland*, 373 U.S. 80 (1963)), by express federal statute, 18 U.S.C. §3500 (the "Jencks Act"), and by the Federal Rules of Criminal Procedure (Rule 16). The Subcommittee finds the FBI's failure to produce the above-noted materials inexcusable.

The Subcommittee is concerned that, even today, officials of the FBI may not be fully cognizant of their constitutional and statutory obligations with regard to criminal discovery. In his testimony to the Subcommittee, one FBI agent asserted his view that the FBI's written critique of the U.S. Marshals Service's actions at Ruby Ridge was not subject to discovery because only "one or two" copies existed, because it constituted "simply opinions," and because the document was not an "official" document since it "was not placed in a file." (10/31/95 Tr. at 170-74 (Dillon)). Those interpretations of law are simply wrong. We expect the FBI to improve the education of its agents in this regard. We further expect that such training will include the reminder that, while the FBI remains free to make recommendations concerning the production of sensitive materials, the ultimate determination of whether such materials must be produced rests with the Office of the United States Attorney.

Delay in producing relevant documents
Several documents clearly relevant to the charges in the criminal trial against Randy Weaver and Kevin Harris were not produced by the FBI until well after the trial had commenced, and only then arrived via fourth-class U.S. mail. These documents included materials related to the FBI Shooting Incident Review Report, and in particular notes on interviews of the Hostage Rescue Team and two drawings by Agent Horiuchi concerning the circumstances of the shots taken by him at Ruby Ridge.

The FBI agent responsible for facilitating document requests between the USAO and FBI Headquarters testified that the prosecutors and FBI case agents were surprised by the production of these documents during trial, since they had "simply forgotten" that defense attorneys had requested such documents by a subpoena nearly two months before. (10/13/95 Tr. at 110 (Dillon)). The FBI Headquarters agent responsible for gathering and producing these documents testified that he first learned about the subpoena on or about April 14, 1993, requested that the documents be gathered some two weeks later, received them eleven days later, took ten days to review them, and then had them mailed to the prosecution team in Idaho, where they were received on June 4, 1993. (10/13/95 Tr. at 122-25 (Callihan)). **As a result of the government's delayed production of these documents, the court imposed sanctions on the prosecution, and Agent Horiuchi was required to re-appear for testimony at trial, weakening the government's case by further highlighting the government's conduct in causing the tragic death of Vicki Weaver.**

Despite repeated requests by the USAO over a period of several months, FBI Headquarters also actively resisted turning over several documents to the prosecution team on the ground that they were "internal documents" of the FBI. (10/12/95 Tr. at 113-14 (Dillon), 126 (Callihan), 166 (Reynolds)). Agent T. Michael Dillon testified "The U.S. Attorney's Office wanted these documents and we facilitated—forwarded their repeated requests for the documents. FBI Headquarters had another view. The people in FBI Headquarters believed that they weren't necessary." (10/13/95 Tr. at 114 (Dillon)). These documents, including the Shooting Incident Review Report, the FBI's critique of the Marshals Service's actions, and the FBI operations plan for Ruby Ridge, were released by the FBI only after the Department of Justice interceded and directed their release. (10/13/95 Tr. at 127-28, 133 (Dillon), 138-42 (Reynolds)). There is no question that this resistance came in large part from Headquarters and the Section of the FBI headed by Potts and Coulson, high-ranking officials of the FBI who were themselves intimately involved in the FBI's conduct at Ruby Ridge.

The FBI's failure to timely produce discoverable material substantially prejudiced the government's case, resulted in court-imposed penalties, and heightened the public perception that the government was playing fast-and-loose with the truth at Ruby Ridge. The Subcommittee asks the FBI to institute programs to improve the quality of its response to criminal discovery demands, including attention to the organization, coordination and monitoring of discovery requests and responses. The Subcommittee understands that the FBI has already begun this process, by, for example, forming a new Discovery Unit reporting to the General Counsel.

Adversarial relationship with USAO

Both the FBI's withholding of clearly discoverable materials and inexcusable delay in producing such materials are symptomatic of what Assistant Director Potts admitted was a "clear breakdown in the relationship" between the FBI and the USAO. (9/21/95 Tr. at 111 (Potts)). Maurice O. Ellsworth, the United States Attorney in Idaho at the time of the Ruby Ridge incident, has himself severely criticized the FBI for its complete failure of cooperation in the discovery process. (9/15/95 Tr. at 136-38, 148-50 (Ellsworth)). Indeed, Ellsworth informed the Subcommittee of his conclusion that the FBI had delayed or refused to produce relevant information because they "feared that it would embarrass the FBI." (Id. at 165).

Institutional bias

Throughout the course of its many reports, the FBI accorded its own agents undue deference. Their stories were accepted at face value and were only rarely the subject of probing inquiry. FBI agents conducting the reviews vigorously pursued exculpatory leads while passing over inculpatory evidence. For example, members of the Shooting Incident Review Team headed by Agent Thomas Miller failed to press various sniper-observers of the Hostage Rescue Team about the Rules of Engagement they were acting under and the circumstances under which

Agent Lon Horiuchi fired his two shots. Instead, the Review Team simply accepted the Rules of Engagement without questioning their propriety or legality and without inquiring whether the Rules may have had some impact upon the snipers. When asked why the Team did not look into the Rules of Engagement, Agent Miller replied that inquiry into the Rules was not part of his job. (Miller Testimony at 153). Likewise, the Shooting Incident Review Group brushed off any critical evaluation of the Rules of Engagement and their impact on the events at Ruby Ridge. However, any thorough and conscientious inquiry into the circumstances surrounding the shooting death of an innocent civilian must look into the Rules an agent is operating under and his state of mind when firing a shot. The failure to do so regarding Agent Horiuchi is inexcusable.

In contrast to the objective scrutiny we expect from the FBI, the Shooting Incident Review Team did a haphazard job collecting the evidence and analyzing the legal issues. For example, the Report refers to Vicki Weaver as "Vicki Harris" on several occasions. The author of the report dismissed this error as typographic, but it obviously was more than that: it manifests a critical inattention to detail. In addition to the factual errors, the Report reveals a serious misunderstanding of the rules of deadly force. In analyzing the shooting of Vicki Weaver, the Review Team concluded that "the use of deadly force was justified in that she willfully placed herself in harm's way by attempting to assist Harris, and in so doing, overtly contributed to the immediate threat which continued to exist against the helicopter crew and approaching HRT personnel." In fact, there is no evidence to suggest that Vicki Weaver was attempting to assist Kevin Harris in any hostile action. There is no reason to conclude that holding the door open for a retreating subject is any kind of a contribution to an immediate threat. **And even more troubling is the team's conclusion that an innocent party who "place[s] herself in harm's way" can be the subject of deadly force. That conclusion is frighteningly wrong.**

The FBI Inspection Division's Report of its Official Inquiry, prepared under the supervision of Inspector Walsh's team was asked simply to collect the facts and then to present a detailed factual summary to the Department of Justice Task Force reviewing the Ruby Ridge matter. The Task Force, headed by Barbara Berman, was then charged with analyzing the facts gathered by Inspector Walsh's team and drawing conclusions. However, rather than complying with their mandate, members of the Walsh team went out of their way to solicit legal and forensic opinions supporting the FBI's actions at Ruby Ridge. The Walsh team's decision to flout an explicit order from the Justice Department exposes the FBI's defensive attitude toward criticism.

Likewise, during the course of the Administrative Review headed by Agent Charles Mathews, FBI agents failed to probe adequately into the questions of who approved the Rules of Engagement. Agent Eugene Glenn, the on-scene commander at Ruby Ridge and a central participant in the approval of the Rules of Engagement, told our Subcommittee that in the Mathews review he never was even asked who approved those Rules. (9/19/95 Tr. at 15-16 (Glenn)). Members of the Mathews team simply accepted Assistant Director Larry Potts' assertion that he had not approved the Rules of Engagement. **Rather than attempting to uncover and resolve any discrepancies, FBI agents avoided uncomfortable facts.**

Perhaps the most disturbing demonstration of this approach to the Ruby Ridge investigation involves former Assistant Director Larry Potts' notes on the Rules of Engagement. During the Task Force investigation, Potts told his interviewers that he had taken contemporaneous notes during his Ruby Ridge involvement. But he told them that the notes had been turned over to the Violent Crimes/Major Offenders Section of the FBI's Criminal Investigative Division. The Task Force requested the notes but never received them. (Task Force Report at 158 n. 537). The Mathews team does not seem to have made any effort to find the notes. These notes were critically important as one of the few pieces of documentary evidence to shed light on who approved the Rules of Engagement. **The failure of the FBI to find and turn these notes over to the Berman Task Force is as disturbing as it is inexplicable. So is the failure of the FBI to track them**

down until a criminal investigation and a Senate investigation were underway.

Finally, one need look no further than the After Action Report for a demonstration of the protective attitude of FBI agents asked to review their agency's conduct. The After Action report concluded that Ruby Ridge was a "success" and directly attributable to the FBI's actions. In contrast, an FBI agent wrote a harshly critical report of the U.S. Marshals Service after the Ruby Ridge siege ended. The difference between the critical tone of this so-called Marshals' Critique and the self-congratulatory tone of the After Action Report is instructive. The FBI was coddled; other agencies were analyzed and criticized.

The many FBI reports reveal a reluctance on the part of FBI agents to approach a situation like Ruby Ridge with an open mind. Instead, Ruby Ridge seems to have been approached with an unwillingness to find improper conduct on the part of other FBI agents. This aversion is certainly understandable: the FBI is composed of many exceedingly loyal agents, and their loyalty to the organization does the FBI credit and undoubtedly makes it a stronger agency. But the very quality of allegiance which contributes to the rarity of misconduct in the FBI perversely made it more difficult for the FBI to scrutinize itself objectively for misbehavior at Ruby Ridge. Few agents eagerly uncover wrongdoing in their own organization. They do not want to dishonor the FBI. This sympathy is understandable, but it is also unacceptable.

Obviously, not all FBI agents may have this kind of reluctance, and the Department of Justice Office of Professional Responsibility has through its experience identified individual agents who it believes can be relied upon to vigorously investigate their own agency. But the Subcommittee does not believe that successful investigations of the FBI ultimately should turn on whether a DOJ-OPR attorney is able to handpick specific FBI agents who can be relied upon. We believe any attorney at the Justice Department should be able to call upon any FBI agent to objectively investigate the agency.

The Subcommittee notes that the FBI has done an admirable job investigating itself on many prior occasions.

And the Subcommittee has faith in the FBI's continuing ability to investigate and discipline its agents. But adequate and independent oversight of the FBI is crucial to avoid at a minimum, the appearance of institutional bias within the FBI. Such oversight is particularly important in cases like Ruby Ridge, which involve deep-rooted and systemic problems and large numbers of agents from all echelons of the FBI. However, it notes that the problem of institutional bias is particularly acute in cases like Ruby Ridge which involve deep-rooted and systemic problems and large numbers of agents drawn from the highest to the lowest echelons of the FBI—rather than cases which involve isolated agents violating discrete laws.

Inadequate insulation from subjects of review

Many of the FBI agents conducting the internal reviews were not adequately insulated from the subjects of their reviews. The FBI has an Inspection Division and an Office of Professional Responsibility ("FBI-OPR") within that division. FIB agents are assigned to the Inspection Division as part of their career rotation. Thus, agents come into the Division as inspectors or assistant inspectors for a specified period of time and then return to other divisions of the FBI after their tour of duty. These inspectors are required to investigate the FBI's own conduct.

The various Ruby Ridge reports reveal several instances of friends reviewing friends' conduct and the subjects of the reviews later sitting on the promotion boards of the very agents who reviewed their conduct. This has created the impression that a small group of insiders review the conduct of the FBI, punishing lower-level "outsider" FBI agents and protecting higher-level, inside-track FBI agents, Whether the impression is correct or not, the FBI has allowed it to form, thereby harming its own credibility.

For example, Inspector Walsh testified that he considered Assistant Director Potts a friend, while Potts acknowledged that he had a close relationship with Walsh. (9/21/95 tr. at 100 (Walsh)); (9/21/95 Tr. at 94-95 (Potts)). Walsh considered this friendship strong enough to tell his supervisor, Assistant Director David G. Binney, about the relationship. However, Binney told him that it would not be a problem. In addition, Potts sat on Agent Mathews' promotion board after the Mathews Report was completed, and Coulson acknowledged that he considered Mathews— who had been his subordinate for several years—to be a friend of long standing. (9/21/95 Tr. at 93 (Coulson)). Director Freeh had a close relationship with Potts as well. (10/19/95 Tr. at 40 (Freeh)). The Subcommittee does not mean to suggest that simply knowing the subject of an inquiry disqualifies an investigator. However, all of these relationships with Potts went beyond mere acquaintance, raised an appearance of partiality, and ultimately may have contributed to the skewed perspective of the reports.

Moreover, the Subcommittee has reservations about the way that the Inspection Division is structured. It believes that agent-inspectors do the best job that they can and that they are not consciously biased. However, the practice of letting agent-inspectors review the conduct of friends and colleagues is suspect, and the Subcommittee is pleased to see that the FBI has recently implemented a strict refusal policy. It notes, however, that the operation of the refusal process remains to be evaluated. In addition, the FBI should consider whether the practice of rotating agents in and out of the Inspection Division over a short period of time contributes to the appearance of partiality. Agent-inspectors who know that they may shortly have to work with the subjects of their inspections are that the subjects may later sit on their promotion boards are not sufficiently insulated to assure objectivity.

CONCLUSION

The events at Ruby Ridge have helped to weaken the bond of trust that must exist between ordinary Americans and our law enforcement agencies. Those bonds must be reestablished—and that healing must begin with an honest accounting by those in government whose actions and inactions caused the deaths on Ruby Ridge.

It has been the Subcommittee's overriding purpose to demand such accountability—and, in so demanding, to help reestablish the principle that under our constitutional system of government no one is above the law. The reaffirmation of that principle is the means to avoid future Ruby Ridges.

End of excerpts taken from
The Senate Subcommittee Hearings

DRAW YOUR OWN "CONCLUSION"

By Randy and Sara Weaver

After reading the previous pages you have undoubtedly surmised what our conclusions are in regards to the heinous events that took place at Ruby Ridge in August 1992. We could probably write an entire book consisting of our opinions based solely on the Subcommittee's findings. However, rather than giving you more of our feelings on the contradictions and inaction's of the Federal Government, we want you to derive your own conclusions based on the truths that have finally been put in writing for you to read. We feel sure that you, also, will have your own burning questions as to why more actions have not been taken to set the wrongs right. Our loved ones, Vicki and Sam, are gone forever. We can only hope and pray that their lives were not taken in vain.

12

Life After Ruby Ridge

By Sara Weaver

I just didn't know where to fit in. I didn't fit in.

--Sara Weaver

Upon leaving Idaho immediately after the siege, we went to live with our grandparents, Dave and Jean Jordison in Fort Dodge, Iowa. After a few months, taking care of 10-month-old Elisheba became quite a handful for my grandma. My mother's sister, Julie, and her husband, Keith had made the decision to take Rachel, Elisheba and I to live with them in Johnston, Iowa, a suburb of Des Moines. They already had two daughters, Emily and Kelsey, so it was quite a houseful.

It was decided that Rachel and I should go to school. We were both terrified at the thought of going to a public school. We had been home schooled all of our lives, and had no idea what to expect. We both struggled in our first year of public schooling. Academically I did fine; it was socially where I felt like a misfit. I just didn't know where to fit in. I didn't fit in. As a 16-year-old teenager, I didn't know which clothes were cool, or who to hang out with. Johnston was full of rich, snobby kids who were used to the "easy" life. They seemed to look down their noses at me and judge me based on the stories they saw on the evening news or articles they read in newspapers. These stories were often times filled with lies. After all, since we were originally from Iowa, Ruby Ridge was a big story for the local media.

There were mornings when I loathed the idea of getting out of bed to go to school. As I went through the halls I was constantly faced with long stares from kids who just didn't understand, or sympathetic looks from teachers.

I did have one teacher however, that really made a positive impact on me. He teaches art, but he taught me a great deal about life. I will be forever grateful to him. Despite the social struggle, I tried my best and made good grades. I wanted my grades to reflect all my mothers hard work and dedication as my "teacher". I also wanted to make my dad proud of me. I didn't want him to have to worry about us, as he was going through hell as it was.

Dad got out of jail in December of 1993, my senior year in high school. It was an extremely happy reunion and brought me great relief. We had sure missed him. We were all together again and maybe now we could start to piece our life back together.

Rachel and Elisheba went to live with Dad in Grand Junction, Iowa, where his sister Marnis lived. I stayed with Keith and Julie so I could finish my senior year and graduate high school. After graduation, I too moved to Grand Junction to be near my dad. My fiancé David Cooper and I made a down payment on a small house. We lived there for about two years, but I ached to get back to the mountains.

After travelling some and searching for property, we decided to move to northwestern Montana, which is where we are currently living. My dad and sisters have moved out here too. I love it. Montana has neat people, beautiful scenery, fresh air, and the rugged mountains I crave. Once the mountains are in your blood, they're impossible to leave for very long. I will forever be grateful to my parents for raising me in the mountains of The Great Pacific Northwest.

Epilogue

Dealing with the aftermath of Ruby Ridge has been an enormous struggle for our family. Day after day, month after month year after year, we have had to stare it in the face and try to come out on top just to maintain a somewhat "normal" existence.

Our family was so close knit and we were so dependant on each other, that when Vicki and Sam were taken from us, it was as though the fabric of our lives had been torn completely in two, and we had no one to turn to, to mend it. It couldn't be mended. Because we had been spared our lives, we have had to try to go on without them. It has been a tough adjustment for all of us.

Time dulls the pain somewhat, but it never goes away. It's always there, waiting in the wings; ready to take a stab at us when we least expect it. The only way to dissolve the pain would be to totally forget the tragedy. Since that is not an option, we are at times left with feelings of complete helplessness.

We hope that this book will help carry on Sam and Vicki's memories long after we are gone, and the media has forgotten Ruby Ridge. It's the only thing left we can do for them. They deserve to be remembered forever.

The incidents at both Ruby Ridge and Waco need to be remembered. History has a way of repeating itself, and what happened to our family, and the families in Waco, Texas is something we hope and pray never happens to anyone ever again. However, it would be rather naïve and ignorant to think that it *couldn't* ever happen again. Governments have been using and abusing their people for centuries. Who is to say that it will suddenly stop now? Sadly, we really don't think it will.

When a government becomes so large and impersonal that it's agents can literally gas, burn and murder it's own citizens with impunity; that government is doomed.

God grants liberty only to those who love it, and are always ready to guard and defend it.
                                                                —Daniel Webster

UPDATE

(This book had already gone to the printer when the news hit the nation that the manslaughter charges against Lon Horiuchi had been dismissed. We could not let the presses roll on without giving our feelings in regards to this travesty of justice.)

Thursday, May 14, 1998, marks yet another sad day in the wayward course of American history. This is the day that the manslaughter charges brought against Lon Horiuchi, the FBI sniper who shot and killed Vicki, were dismissed based on the supremacy clause. How ironic that the very word they wrongfully "pinned" on me (i.e. Randy Weaver is a "white supremacist") played a key role in having the charges dismissed against a federal murderer.

When we first heard the news, a range of emotions went through us. There was the initial feeling of disappointment and anger. The decision did not come as a complete surprise though. After all, we were already well aware of how unjust our government is in regards to its citizens. Yet, Judge Lodge is the same judge who sat on the bench during our trial and we felt, or had hoped, that he would not be swayed from the truths he had heard during the trial.

This latest government blunder only strengthens our mistrust of the government. We not only feel sadness for our family, but for all Americans. This judgement is a concise statement that, we the people, are of little significance to our present government. Federal agents, who will not have to worry about any legal recourse, can snuff us out at any time.

This decision *can* be appealed. We will surely encourage the Boundary County Prosecutor to do so. There still remains a flicker of hope inside us that someday justice will prevail. We have to keep that small flame going, for if we let it die, then Vicki and Sam's deaths will have been for naught.

Bibliography

Allen, Gary. *None Dare Call It Conspiracy.* Seal Beach, California: Concord Press, 1971.

Gritz, Colonel James "Bo". *Called to Serve.* Lazarus, 1991.

Orwell, George. *Nineteen Eighty-Four.* Signet Classic, 1949

Rand, Ayn. *Atlas Shrugged.* Signet, 1957.

Ross, John. *Unintended Consequences.* St. Louis, Missouri: Accurate Press, 1996

Wolfe, Claire. *101 Things To Do Till The Revolution.* Port Townsend, Washington: Loompanics Unlimited, 1996

Woodrow, Ralph. *Babylon Mystery Religion.* 1966.

Senate Hearings. *The Federal Raid On Ruby Ridge, ID.* Washington: U.S. Government Printing Office, 1997